literacy con cariño

*The ways in which literacy*
*is thought about*
*in this country are*
*reductive and dangerous.*
*In their application,*
*they narrow the range*
*of pedagogy and suppress*
*the possibilities of research.*
*This is the real literacy crisis.*

Stuckey, *The Violence of Literacy*

# literacy con cariño

## a story of migrant children's success

## new edition

**Curtis W. Hayes**
Boise State University

**Robert Bahruth**
Boise State University

**Carolyn Kessler**
The University of Texas at San Antonio

Heinemann
Portsmouth, NH

**Heinemann**
A division of Reed Elsevier Inc.
361 Hanover Street
Portsmouth, NH 03801–3912
http://www.heinemann.com

*Offices and agents throughout the world*

© 1998 by Curtis W. Hayes, Robert Bahruth, and Carolyn Kessler

Library of Congress Cataloging-in-Publication Data
Hayes, Curtis W.
    Literacy con cariño : a story of migrant children's success /
Curtis W. Hayes, Robert Bahruth, Carolyn Kessler. — New ed.
     p.   cm.
    Includes bibliographical references (p. 159).
    ISBN 0-325-00007-7 (alk. paper)
    1. Children of migrant laborers—Education—Texas—Case studies.
    2. Mexican American children—Education—Texas—Case studies.
    3. Language experience approach in education—Texas—Case studies.
    4. Education, Bilingual—Texas—Case studies.    I. Bahruth, Robert.
II. Kessler, Carolyn.    III. Title.
LC5152.T4H39   1998
371.826'24—DC21                        98-8505
                                          CIP

Editors: William Varner and Janine Duggan
Production: Elizabeth Valway
Cover design: Jenny Greenleaf
Manufacturing: Louise Richardson

Printed in the United States of America on acid-free paper
02 01 00 99     DA      3 4 5

*To the children of August—*
*the migrant children*
*of South Texas—who,*
*with their parents, taught us*
*much about teaching,*
*learning, and caring.*
*¡Vayan con dios nuestros*
*estudiantes y amigos!*

# contents

# acknowledgments

The following friends and colleagues contributed to the writing of this revision:

In particular, many thanks to Bill Varner and Janine Duggan, our editors at Heinemann.

Our deep appreciation as well to Marialice Hayes—teacher, wife, and friend—for her many hours of reading through the revised manuscript and providing thoughtful and insightful comments and criticisms.

For their continual support we thank Guisela Bahruth and Mary Ellen Quinn.

Donaldo Macedo brought *Literacy con Cariño* to the attention of Paulo Freire: Con cariño y gratitude por sus palabras de un maestro que entendió.

# foreword

In choosing the title *Literacy con Cariño*, the authors of this timely and important book present us with an announcement that requires that we, as readers, take distance from the traditional mechanistic world view that falsely dichotomizes the subject from the object, the theory from the practice, breaking apart their dialectical unity. It is no coincidence that Curtis Hayes, Robert Bahruth, and Carolyn Kessler begin the introduction to their book explaining that "*Literacy con Cariño* is curious linguistically because it mixes two languages." In reality, this code switching becomes an object of curiosity only for those who have unreflectively embraced the false dichotomization of realities. For the students who are studied in this book, who are exposed to both English and Spanish, and possess various degrees of mastery of both languages, code switching represents a process of meaning-making shaped by the constant juggling of two worlds, two cultures, and two languages. In other words, the title *Literacy con Cariño* requires that we make an effort to understand as fully as we can—an effort not simply to understand the reading of each of the constituent words of the title but to comprehend more deeply the force of reading that each individual word requires when it is inserted in a web of relationships.

The lack of understanding of students' intimate, yet fragile relationship involving two languages and two cultures is, perhaps, responsible for the students' so-called reading and writing problems. As the authors correctly point out, the understanding of the teaching context invariably involves "more than books to be assigned and read, content areas to be mastered and tested." The authors of *Literacy con Cariño* also understand that "teaching entails a mutual as well as reciprocal act, a collaboration." Such collaboration, as exemplified in *Literacy con Cariño*, points to dialogism, which is a requirement of human nature and also a sign of the educator's democratic stand. There is no communication without dialogism, and communication lies at the core of the vital phenomenon. That is, communication is life and a vector for more life. However, communication cannot occur in a language that students cannot understand. That is why Robert Bahruth, the teacher, while understanding the importance of teaching English to his students, also understands that "proficiency in English should not be at the expense of their first language and culture."

The authors of *Literacy con Cariño* deeply understand the pedagogical and political implications of not sacrificing the students' native language. The immediate recognition of familiar worlds and experiences enhances the development of a positive self-concept in children who are somewhat insecure about the status of their language and culture. In this sense, the students' language is the only means by which they can develop their own voice, a prerequisite to the development of a positive sense of self-worth. This is why Robert Bahruth's classroom "encompasse[d] more than just reading and writing, in Spanish or in English. . . . Robert became an advocate of the children's efforts—he applauded, he cheered, he urged on, he commiserated with them when things did not go exactly right, and he celebrated when things did."

*Literacy con Cariño* also announces a departure from the production and reproduction of false dichotomies—English-Spanish, theory-practice—by demonstrating that the task of a teacher, who is also a learner, should be both joyful and rigorous. It demands seriousness and scientific, physical, emotional, and affective preparation. As Robert Bahruth so effectively demonstrated, it is impossible to teach without the capacity to love your students even if it means being called ridiculous, silly, or unscientific. In short, *Literacy con Cariño* underscores the important fact which is often dismissed by technicist educators that we study, we learn, we teach, and we know with our entire body. We do all of these things with feeling, with emotion, with wishes, with fear, with doubts, with passion, and also with critical reasoning. However, we never study, learn, teach, or know with the last only. *Literacy con Cariño* makes it abundantly clear that we should never dichotomize cognition and emotion. Such ideological separation between, for instance, English and Spanish, between text and context, between an object and its raison d'être, implies regrettable error; it involves truncating the learners' epistemological curiosity.

Instead of depositing the teacher's knowledge in a lockstep, with routinized and boring memorization of facts, the experiment analyzed in *Literacy con Cariño* provides us with an understanding of what it means to emphasize an epistemologically curious posture as fundamental in constituting the theoretical context that informs our practice as educators. Thus, it is also an error to negate theory in our practice, as some educators, almost proudly, boast that they do not do theory. What these educators do not realize is that in negating theory in favor of practice, they are invariably involved in a form of bad theory versus a good theory, which challenges both the teachers' and the learners' naive curiosity so they can develop a more rigorous and critical awareness of their teaching and learning practice.

*Literacy con Cariño* is an important testimony of how progressive teachers can reject a technicist vision of education in which all that really matters is technical training, the standardization of content, and the transfer of a well-behaved knowledge to the learners. This approach to education not only dulls the epistemological curiosity of both teachers and learners, but it also ignores the intelligence and creativity of learners. It is the intelligence and creativity of learners coupled with the teacher's critical, rigorous, and loving methodology that gives meaning to engaging in *Literacy con Cariño*.

Paulo Freire and Donaldo Macedo

# introduction

## to the new edition

*Observing linguistic human rights
implies at an individual level
that everyone can identify positively
with their mother tongue,
and have that identification
respected by others,
irrespective of whether
their mother tongue is
a minority or a majority language.*

Skutnabb-Kangas, *Linguistic Human Rights:
Overcoming Linguistic Discrimination*

Six years have elapsed since the publication of the first edition of *Literacy con Cariño*, and in those years we have had time to reflect on what we said then as well as on what we want to say now in the new edition. Our observations follow, attesting to changes in our children, ourselves, and our subject.

We have changed as teachers and researchers; we have read more, met and listened to more students and teachers, and visited and worked in more classrooms. We see situations in our teaching and in our students' learning differently. Our students reflect on their learning, either by commenting on a classmate's work or by commenting on their own. For example, Larry (whom you will meet in Chapter 3) writes on the last page of his first journal:

*Do you remember the first day I didn't write just like one line? I like writing in my journal.*

And in *Make-Believe Bestiaries*, Larry writes about the "Liuck," an animal that can "kill" Francisco's "Tigebear." But it is Apolinar who has the last laugh: He reads both stories and writes one of his own, a story about the "Cheetahcat" which "kills" both "Liucks" and "Tigebears." We continue to marvel at those episodes and the children's renewal of their interest in school. Larry, the child who doesn't write, becomes a writer. The children are incredibly able. In a relatively poor school district, they receive little in the way of resources, but some teachers do much with much; our children do much "con nada."

We share a number of experiences in this edition from that year in 1983–1984 because we believe that they will help teachers build on what their students can do and what they can learn. Although all three of us recognize the importance of capable and effective teachers, we recognize we don't teach as much as the children learn: We provide the catalysts, spaces for learning, and critical questioning. To do so requires careful, thorough planning and continual reflection about how the day, the week, the month are going and how we may improve.

We are always in the process of teaching and learning; we represent "an unquiet pedagogy" in flux (Freire 1991). We no longer succumb to the rigidity of a scope and sequence, or a linear-sequential curriculum, with the teaching day chopped into discrete hours and minutes assigned to one subject or another: math from 8:30 to 9:30, P.E. from 9:30 to 10, followed by reading from 10 to 11, and so on. The teaching day is seamless, and we take the time needed. If we need to read and write a complete day, we read and write a complete day. Most importantly, we extend the time normally spent on reading and writing and strongly believe this extension is a major key to success.

Today as we continue to teach in bilingual classes, every subject is touched upon but at various levels during the week. We don't ignore; we integrate. We are ever mindful of "teachable moments" and of the children's interests and concerns. We are knowledgeable about what students need to learn.

We look back on our experiences as evolutionary. We ask our readers to view us as teachers learning, from the time we begin with the alphabet (the "capítulares") to the final papers the students write. We include ourselves in the activities we assign by writing alongside our students. And as we write and as we prepare to write, we all learn a great deal about developing knowledge, which we can see, for example, in the experimental science papers written here. Looking at those papers now, we see that the children write "wrong" before they write conventionally.

*Literacy con Cariño* is an example of school reform and renewal, and we see it in the changing attitudes of the children, who learn after years of being failed by traditional schooling.

A movement for change is in its nascent stages in America's classrooms, fanned by teachers who have shifted focus from method to philosophy. Teachers are beginning to look beyond buzzwords and bandwagons and the current fad. They are abandoning the language of deficit and remediation. Through research and conversations with their peers and many times with their students, they are transcending the past and today are reaching a deeper knowledge of and appreciation for their vocation. Teachers are beginning to speak the language of possibilities. They neither blame the child for not learning, nor do they blame themselves, but they teach until the child learns.

*Literacy con Cariño* is a map of how we change, and we wish to invite teachers who are considering change to journey with us, to read the story of how we, with our children, become learners.

One of the seminal pieces in kindling our transformation is the late Paulo Freire's article "The Importance of the Act of Reading." The eloquence and poetry of Freire's ideas are not lost in this paraphrase from Portuguese: A teacher creates an environment for learning, Freire says, which builds upon the knowledge and experience that a child brings to the classroom. The relationship between parents as teachers and the school is not only critical but nurturing. Learning is endemic: Teachers cannot prevent a child from learning if the learning is tied to the experiences of a child's life and the child's learning contributes to a sense of self-worth. The school's world must be matched with the child's world. Freire (1983) writes,

*My parents introduced me to reading the word at a certain moment in this rich experience of understanding my immediate world. Deciphering the word flowed naturally from **reading** my particular world; it was not something superimposed on it. I learned to read and write on the ground of the backyard of my house, in the shade of the mango trees, with the words from my world rather* *than from the wider world of my parents.*

> *When I arrived at Eunice Vascancello's private school, I was already literate. Eunice continued and deepened my parents' work. With her, reading the word, the phrase, and the sentence never entailed a break with reading the* **world**. *With her, reading the word meant reading the* **word-world**. *(8)*

Freire claims that he could not "reduce" learning to words, syllables, and letters, which is,

> *a process of teaching in which the teacher* **fills** *the supposedly* **empty** *heads of learners with his or her words. On the contrary, the student is the subject of the process of learning to read and write as an act of knowing and of creating. The fact that he or she needs the teacher's help, as in any pedagogical situation, does not mean that the teacher's help nullifies the student's creativity and responsibility for constructing his or her own written language and for reading this language.*

And, finally, "The teacher cannot put it together for the student; that is the student's creative task" (10).

Freire's observations instruct us: The parents of the children, although literate in the world, may not be capable in the written world and unable to provide an introduction to literacy similar to the one Freire's parents provided for him. The parents "read" the world of crops, fields, weather, and highways—a literacy critical to their survival. A teacher's challenge is to connect the written word to a world that children know how to "read." As Eunice did so many years ago for Paulo, we saw the value in connecting the children's literacy with the literacy required by the school by redefining literacy itself. The children's parents understood how failure to understand their "literacy" contributes to the withholding of literacy from their children, who are so ready and eager to learn.

In our revision we excise language that was *acritical*. For example, we wrote in 1991 that *we* "empowered" students through the activities we practiced in the classroom. We now believe that *we* cannot empower students; students can only empower *themselves*—which they do by understanding their world and grappling with it. We learned from their papers that is exactly what occurred. They became more aware of what they had to do to live in their world and how they could use their literacy to take advantage of education to move beyond the fields in which they and their parents worked.

Through reflecting we have learned a great deal between the first edition and the revised. We would continue to have our students write in English and Spanish—and even increase the time spent on Spanish language-arts. As has been pointed out (Freire and Macedo, 1987; Cummins, 1994), the path to literacy is through the child's first language. Second, we would now do more transactional (content area) writing, critical thinking, and metacognitive discussion, employing both languages in order to speed up the process of the acquisition of literacy. Even so, the children experience an average three-year gain in literacy and emerge with literacy skills in both languages. While both Spanish and English are of equal status in the academic discourse of the classroom, the children would be passing to the middle school the following year, where there is no bilingual program and English is the language of instruction. Our goal was to prepare them for the demands of an all-English learning environment. That all graduated— albeit four did so with their GEDs—with some enrolled in honors classes, substantiates what we accomplished together as a community of learners.

# introduction
*to the first edition*

Collaboration. All educators would agree that universities and school districts can mutually benefit from it. The project that we describe in this book is the result of informal collaboration between a classroom teacher of bilingual children and two university professors. Ideally, reciprocity is what teacher education is about. A teacher enrolls in classes in a university or college to learn strategies, theories, and research that may be helpful. He or she returns to the classroom to try out, and perhaps implement, what has been learned. The university professor, also engaged in teaching, may visit and receive feedback from the teacher and his or her students, and in this way learns what works in practice and revises or discards what doesn't.

*Literacy con Cariño* began when a fifth-grade teacher returned to a university to earn a certificate required to teach limited-English-proficient (LEP) children. Robert Bahruth had been assigned by his district to teach a group of bilingual children who, primarily because of inadequate literacy, had not known school success. The story became one of collaboration between this teacher and two of his university professors, Curt Hayes and Carolyn Kessler. Robert asked them to help him organize his classroom and to provide a sounding board during the school year—and to visit his classroom from time to time. Both said yes. But the realization that this was a collaboration came toward the end of the school year; and only at the end of the school year did we realize that what we had inadvertently conceived and implemented might also be helpful to other teachers who struggle in their search for strategies and methods to help these children. Collaboration is not new in education. But it can be a crucial factor in empowerment—for teachers and students at all levels.

We begin with the reason for our title. *Literacy con Cariño* is curious linguistically because it mixes two languages. It has meaning because our story is about a classroom of bilingual children. Code switching is common in the home language of the students who are the main focus of our collaboration. A deeper dimension encompassed in the title is revealed when the words are examined individually. It is no coincidence that *Literacy* is in English. English is certainly the language of mobility and power in the United States, as well as the world, and English literacy is therefore of primary importance if we are to open the doors of opportunity for our students. Yet the major educational achievement of our students, proficiency in English, should not be at the expense of their first language and culture.

Just as it is intentional that *Literacy* is in English, it is symbolic that *con Cariño* is in Spanish. Attention to caring about and valuing each student individually was the result of a conscious attempt to incorporate into the school culture the affection and caring the students experienced in their homes. Although many of the parents of these children were non-readers, their home lives often reflected rich oral traditions, deeply felt care and love, and a strong desire on the part of the parents for their children to succeed in school. The use of Spanish along with English in our title also reflects the underlying philosophy that prompted Robert to restructure his classroom around activities that provided the focus for the school day: reading and writing.

Our title thus parallels our goal of literacy achieved through a nurturing process. Attending to affective concerns, undoing the learned helplessness students brought with them to the classroom after years of failure, and demonstrating personal literacy all hold promise for students with a history of failure. By looking for strengths in his students, Robert found them and built on them.

Our title also traces a journey, and it encompasses more than just reading and writing, in Spanish or in English. Not just another teaching method, ours is a story of advocacy. Robert became an advocate of the children's efforts—he applauded, he cheered, he urged on, he commiserated with them when things did not go exactly right, and he celebrated when things did. Students were empowered during this one year to teach themselves—they talked and wrote about their lives outside the walls of the classroom, about what they were learning and the effect their learning would have on their lives. The journey was not merely an enriching experience for them, but for the three of us as well. During the year we became more than teachers. In fact, we strengthened our own notions of what teaching is. Teaching is more than books to be assigned and read, content areas to be mastered and tested. Teaching entails a mutual as well as reciprocal act, a collaboration.

The reciprocal act was not evident in Robert's teaching the year before. A first-year teacher in the district, he had just returned to the United States after having taught English for the International School Services in Central America. He assigned readings from fifth-grade textbooks that his students had difficulty comprehending. He followed the authors' suggestions on how to use the basal readers, working with question-and-answer cards and requiring his students to answer in complete sentences. At the end of the year, although the children had made, on the average, one year's progress in reading proficiency (as measured by the Sucher [1982] Informal Reading Inventory test employed by the district), more progress than they had made in the three previous years taken together, they were still not on grade level, and time was running out for them in terms of educational success. Time was also running out for the children that Robert met the following fall. It was after his first year of teaching that Robert began his studies at the university, looking for ways to help the at-risk children in his care.

Robert began his second year by starting each class day with a story hour. The class favorite, which they asked him to read a number of times, was "The Onion," extracted from Dostoyevski's *The Brothers Karamazov*. He also read or told stories by O. Henry, Saki, Tolstoy, and de Maupassant. In addition, Robert read in Spanish from Juan Sauvageau's *Stories That Must Not Die*, a collection of Hispanic folktales. Basals continued to be part of the curriculum, but the practice of asking factual recall questions about what the students had read was discontinued. Instead, Robert asked them to write about the stories from their basals, the stories he had read to them, and the stories they may have been reading from library books. A number of these writings are in their dialogue journals (see Chapter 3). Robert witnessed a growing appreciation for books and literature, an anticipation of his responses in their journals, and an improved writing ability.

Writing consumed a large part of the school day. The children wrote daily in their journals. They wrote papers about what they were reading and learning. They began to publish classmade books, an activity that made their writing available not only to Robert but also to their classmates. In his text *Writing: Teachers and Children at Work* (1983) Donald H. Graves shares the powerful results achieved when children write and display their work in class-published books. Robert and his students began their publishing venture with a book with lots of student art and little language. The children's enthusiasm for writing increased with the publication of that first book. And with each subsequent book, they became more meticulous about their writing. Editing and spelling improved, as well as the writing itself.

These class-published books supplemented the required basals in that the children wrote about what they were learning.

## Testing

Testing of reading comprehension in the district was measured by the Informal Reading Inventory (Sucher 1982). The IRI was administered at the end of each grading period (six weeks) by the Title I and/or the Title VII reading supervisors. While all reading evaluations have their limitations, the IRI was convenient and, as the year wore on, a revealing instrument by which to gauge the children's progress.

In the test, a child is asked to read aloud for a specified time. The examiner then multiplies by two the number of words read in any thirty-second block and determines the number of miscues or words that have not been decoded accurately. (Eighty percent word recognition is considered the minimum necessary to ensure comprehension.) Finally, five district-prepared comprehension questions are asked, including three factual recall questions, one inference question, and one prediction question. The student has to respond correctly to a minimum of four of the five questions to indicate a satisfactory level of comprehension.

According to the instructions provided by the district's reading coordinator, students read at the instructional level if they read a minimum of eighty words per minute, with eighty percent word recognition, and with eighty percent accuracy on the responses to the questions. If the child reads below eighty percent he or she is considered to be reading at the frustration level, and is having difficulty reading the basal. Various levels of grade-level reading proficiency can be measured in this way, as we shall see.

At the beginning of the year not one of the students that Robert taught reached grade-level norms. Many of them read three to four years below grade level, some were illiterate.

Although we recognize that the IRI criteria are not in accord with many reading and testing theorists and practitioners, the district required that each child's reading proficiency be measured by the use of the IRI as supplied by the publisher, and Robert abided by district rules. The ultimate test for school district purposes was documentation indicating grade-level reading and improvement at the end of the school year—in other words, how well the students could read a basal.

Of course, Robert, in his day-to-day teaching, observed what books the children were checking out, what they said about what they read, and what they wrote about. Good teachers, we believe, know where their children are in terms of comprehension. Anecdotal evidence as well as IRI scores were employed to measure growth—and the children were, as the year progressed, becoming more proficient not only in reading but also in writing.

## The classroom

Robert's room arrangement was different from the one used the previous year. Tables replaced stationary desks. Children sat at these tables in groups, approximately four or five to a table. The class day was structured, with times set aside for math, social studies, science, reading, writing, and other required curriculum components.

Each morning, Robert began with a story hour. He told stories or read from trade books. On Fridays, he would read passages from five books he had purchased or brought from the library; the students could then take these books home over the weekend. Not a single book was lost during the year, and each child was able at least once to take home a book from which Robert had read.

A mailbox was provided for each student (these were made from one-gallon milk containers, cut off at the top). Within, the children kept their notes to Robert and their journals. The children were also urged to correspond with each other. A portion of the story hour was given over to writing in journals and to reading from their basal. During the last fifteen minutes of this first hour, the children could read from books that Robert kept in the classroom or from books they had checked out of the library.

The second hour was devoted to writing. During the writing hour, Robert held short conferences with several students, a different set each day, asking them what they were writing about, how their writing was going, and whether they needed any help getting started or revising what they had already written. Time was also set aside during which they read their writing to their classmates at their table or sometimes to the entire class, usually during sharing time on Friday. Children wrote about what they knew (expressive writing), about what they were learning in social studies and science, and about what they read in language arts.

Robert concluded the day as he had begun, continuing a story he had started in the morning.

A number of teachers have asked how his teaching day differed from the previous year. Robert emphasizes the similarities: having a structure, reading from basals, and following district guidelines on what should be taught. Yet the day was different, especially his expectations of it. Robert was convinced that these children could learn more, progress further, and be led to believe in themselves—

that they were successful learners. The following chapters give evidence that these expectations were justified.

Throughout this book Robert gives indications of the ways his teaching methods are changing, and we return to the reasons why the year succeeded in our last chapter. But most of all we wish to leave our readers with the sense that teaching is something wondrous. The experiences detailed in this text were "heady," exciting. All of us talked to our colleagues, to our friends and spouses, to anyone who would listen about what we were doing during the year and what was happening as we watched Robert teaching and his students learning. Nancie Atwell (1987) captures the essence and perhaps the spirit of our experiences perfectly: "This is the sheer joy of it. I will be surprised every day I teach" (255).

Our story chronicles our surprises and our joys as teachers—whether at the graduate level or of the fifth grade.

# chapter

## *Robert holds*
## *new expectations*

*Sensitivity: the absence of any expectation
that learning will not take place or that it
will be difficult. Where does sensitivity come from?
Every child is born with it.
Children do not need to be taught that they can learn; they
have this implicit expectation
which they demonstrate in their earliest learning about language and about the world.
Experience teaches them that they have limitations,
and unfortunately, experience often teaches them this unneces-
sarily. Children believe their brains
are all-potent until they learn otherwise.*

Frank Smith, *Essays Into Literacy*

*Literacy con Cariño: A Story of Migrant Children's Success* addresses the enormous reading and writing needs of twenty-two children, fifth graders, many of them Spanish dominant, attending school in a small agricultural community in South Texas. The community is the home of a large group of Mexican American laborers who, from spring until early fall, move from place to place, planting, tending, and harvesting crops. The children in our story are the sons and daughters of these laborers. When they arrived for the school year, they were performing significantly below grade-level norms on district tests. Many did not read or write at all. They were the children destined to continue to fail, eventually to drop out of school to join their parents and older brothers and sisters in the fields.

As the families returned to South Texas during those hot days in August and September, the children began to trickle back to school. Their ages—ten through sixteen—did not reflect the age range typically found in a fifth-grade classroom. Many had been retained in grade level at least one year, some more than one. Some had not attended school for a year or two. Others had only recently emigrated from Mexico. Accustomed to failure, they seemed to expect to fail. Our first pedagogical goal had to be to rekindle their "sensitivity." At the end of the school year, they would again accompany their parents as they followed the migrant laborer's path, living in shacks with no running water or indoor toilets, working from sunup to sundown.

Robert Bahruth (from here on Robert or Mr. B.), the fifth-grade teacher, observed immediately the frustration, resignation, and hostility toward school that his students exhibited. He decided the traditional way of presenting the curriculum would not work; yet he knew he must cover the curriculum as mandated by the state and district. If his students were to stay in school rather than drop out, they had to begin to experience success in school, especially in

# one

learning to read and write English. Without education, without the ability to read and write, they would not learn and eventually would have few alternatives or opportunities other than working in the fields.

The experience of this one year details a dramatic change. By May, these students were reading and writing. They had learned not only how to believe in themselves but how to teach themselves and each other. They had learned the required curriculum and were promoted to the sixth grade. Their aspirations and career goals had changed—they were confident. As they left for the fields that summer and said their good-byes, they expressed their eagerness for school to resume in the fall. How and why they succeeded, after years of failure, is our story.

Robert provided appropriate linguistic models and took every opportunity to expose these students to language: interesting, relevant, comprehensible language. Children learn, Frank Smith (1983) says, "by making sense of what are essentially meaningful situations" (9), and these meaningful situations were within the books that Robert read aloud daily. Reading is crucial at any stage of language and writing development. Books, for instance, display all the grammatical structures and discourse rules necessary for writing (Edelsky 1981; Smith 1982; Benitez 1985; Fox 1987). Robert supplied and read from paperbacks containing favorite children's stories and poetry, and in reading stories mirroring their interests and experiences, he provided optimal language input. With this input they began to absorb the conventions of writing—in this case expressive writing, writing that comes from within (Britton 1982; Kirby and Liner, with Vinz 1988).

Robert also exchanged journal entries with the students (see Chapter 3). Together they published books on a variety of topics and content areas. By May, the children had not only made substantial progress in reading and writing proficiency, they had also made substantial gains on state-mandated tests designed to measure academic achievement and knowledge. They had learned to succeed in school, acquired literate skills, and were on their way to becoming life-long learners.

In the following chapters we indicate a rationale for the activities and strategies employed in developing the children's reading and writing proficiency, and we include examples of their writing that corroborate their growth.

In Chapter 2, we introduce the children. We describe a number of their prior experiences—their previous lack of success in learning to read and write sufficiently well to perform school tasks. We cite the attitudes and expectations of some of their past teachers.

In Chapter 3 we encounter Larry's reluctance to engage in dialogue journal exchanges. The class was asked to write in a daily journal. Writing journals about their experiences encouraged the children to write honestly and, at the same time, fluently. Journals were their first expressive writing activity. A few children, Larry foremost among them, were hesitant at first to commit any of their thoughts to paper, but gradually their reluctance disappeared. Soon they wrote more than the required three sentences or lines. Robert responded to their entries with entries of his own. By exchanging entries, the children came to know Robert and he them. The journal entries revealed their likes and dislikes, the books they were reading, the books they preferred to have read to them, and information of a personal, familiar nature. In their journals we also see the children making their first attempts to write about the curriculum, about what they were learning.

"Christina Finds Play in Writing" is the title we've given to Chapter 4. Children enjoy experimenting and playing with language. In spite of their past failure with language and school, these children were no exception. Five playful writing activities each resulted in a class-published collection of their efforts.

While Robert suggested writing topics from time to time, he also let the class "brainstorm" about possible subjects. This led to the writing across the curriculum—about Texas and other states, about foreign countries, about science—that is described in Chapter 5. Topics on states and countries served to widen the children's knowledge of the world and entailed reading, researching, and learning about demographics, geography, geology, and biology. The school's curriculum was thus integrated with reading and writing. (The titles of the books the class published using these writings include *Uncle Sam's Biography* and *International Alphabet Soup*.) The children also discovered nature's wonders. They did research, collected data, described a procedure for "finding out about" what they had collected, and eventually wrote reports on their discoveries. Each new report became more accurate and scientific. And these too were published in class-made books. Gilbert was indeed discovering pieces of the world.

"Florencia Dreams New Dreams" is the title of our final chapter. During the latter part of the academic year, after they had read autobiographies by and biographies of famous people, the children decided to write about themselves, their past, and their goals. They contributed papers to a book they entitled *Great Expectations* (a book about their futures) and to *The Autobiographies of Not-Yet-Famous People*. And great expectations these not-yet-famous students had! For the first time in their lives, they had experienced success during a school year. The Informal Reading Inventory test given at the end of the year by Title I and Title VII supervisors measured an average growth of three years, a phenomenal recovery from past failures and a strong indication of success.

The children of our story have moved on. Almost all advanced to senior high school and graduated, while some received their GEDs; most are doing well (see Epilogue); and many are employed in jobs beyond the fields.

But what worked? Why did education work for these students when it had not worked previously? We believe we know and can list a number of attributes of learning that the children exhibited during this year. Reading and writing remain a significant part of many of their lives. Robert continues to keep up with them through correspondence; they write and he responds. Their reading and writing are ongoing and continual. They have discovered and appreciate the utility of literacy in their daily lives.

# chapter

## The child of August
## starts fifth grade

*Whether in nature or in human relationships,*
*few images are more compelling*
*than that of an encounter:*
*a butterfly and a flower come together*
*in a brief burst of color,*
*the sun's rays and raindrops joined in a rainbow,*
*a mother reaching out for her newborn child,*
*two pairs of eyes held in a deeply felt gaze,*
*two hands clasped in friendship.*
*And surely, among the most meaningful encounters,*
*the one between a child and a book.*

Alma Flor Ada, *A Magical Encounter*

The terrific heat of South Texas in late August makes classroom life hard and uncomfortable, even miserable, especially in poor school districts. Windows remain open to invite whatever breeze there is. Teachers bring their own fans since many schools are not air conditioned. The first cold spell, a "norther," will not arrive until October or November, maybe even December. It was in this situation that Robert found himself, greeting his students on the Monday of the last week in August, the beginning of the school year for most of Texas. His class, eventually to number more than twenty, was there, waiting resignedly—fifth graders, bilingual, attending school in a small, poor, rural South Texas community.

Alex was thirteen, Gilbert twelve (and labeled learning disabled); Francisco was a year older than his sister Patricia, who was eleven. Florencia and Lisa were twelve; Rene was eleven. Norma and Irma were the oldest, fourteen and sixteen respectively. The remainder were age ten, within the normal range of fifth-grade students. The older students had not all been held back: several had stayed out of school for a year or two because their families needed the income they earned working in the fields; and several had recently arrived from Mexico and were placed in the fifth grade because it was the last bilingual grade level in the district. The middle school, beginning with grade six, did not offer bilingual instruction.

From the records of previous years, Robert learned that student absenteeism had been high and that achievement was significantly below grade-level norms on district tests. Some read at the primer (or grade one) level. Others did not read or write at all. Only one student read above grade two, and she read at the grade-four level. They were truly at risk; predictably, many would be squeezed out (Bahruth 1987). Projections based on statistics for the area showed that fewer than fifty percent

# two

would graduate from high school. Their future was limited. Just as inequality can be a cause of alienation, failure can destroy human dignity and self-esteem. These children were bright and capable and their being able to read and write was essential if their futures were to extend and expand.

### Being taught—Not!

The school district's bilingual education program was for children experiencing difficulty in mainstream, English-only classes. Some bilingual teachers taught exclusively in Spanish, some primarily in English, some in both. For instance, students could be taught in their native language one year, English the next, and perhaps in both the year after that.

Year by year, these students fell further and further behind. Most teachers did not want them in their classes because of their history of past failure and the prognosis for more of the same. Teachers did not want to teach "failures," whether in Spanish or in English, for fear of being labeled ineffective or failures themselves. Students who do not learn and who do not do well on tests reflect badly on their teachers.

One of the criteria on which the teachers in the district were evaluated was the number of students who were promoted. One teacher, master's degree in hand, refused to teach bilingual children. Asked why, she said bilingual children could not learn as quickly. Since the district was located in a small town, where everybody knew everybody, she did not want to risk being labeled a poor teacher because the bilingual children were unable to keep up with mainstream, nonbilingual students. The pervasive attitude was that failure among lower-socioeconomic-status bilingual children was normal and inevitable. "Of course they are doing poorly," a teacher commented. "They're bilingual."

Expectations were low. In an exchange with one teacher Robert questioned her approach to teaching bilingual children how to read. She replied, "But this is the way we've always done it."

Robert then asked, "And do you feel it is working?"

She replied, "Of course. They are slowly learning how to read."

Robert persisted: "Would you be satisfied with the same slow progress if they were your own children?"

Her response? "My children aren't bilingual."

The teachers were correct: the fifth-grade limited-English-proficient children were far below grade level. At the first of the year some did not know the alphabet in either their first or their second language. One of their former teachers complained about how intellectually dull this class was because they could not learn how to alphabetize up to the second letter, even though she had taught the skill several times. Many of the children did not know the differences between a city, county, state, and country. They were falling behind because they could not read or write well enough to complete required assignments.

Robert believed his first task was to convince his students they were already successful learners.

## The children

We have arranged our discussion according to the IRI reading scores from the previous May. We begin with the lowest:

**Maria Stella** (age ten), sweet, quiet, and shy, supposedly read at the preprimer stage at the beginning of the year, but in truth she could not read. Her mother, a migrant ("my mother doesn't get vacations"), took an active interest in her education, often visiting the classroom and talking with Robert about what Maria Stella was doing, what she was reading and writing about, what her interests were, and whether she was learning.

**David** (also age ten) had another of the lowest reading scores and not surprisingly a low self-concept. He was listed officially as reading at the primer level, but, like Maria, he could not read. His mother (a migrant) and father (a truck driver during the winter) came to see Robert on several occasions and expressed their concern over David's lack of progress. David had strengths, however, that he would capitalize on: he was an excellent artist, and he used his talents to illustrate stories and covers of class-published books.

**Norma** (fourteen) and **Irma** (sixteen) were older, recent emigrants from Mexico. Their parents were both illiterate migrants. They were placed in this class because it was the highest bilingual grade level. Both knew how to read in Spanish, yet Norma ("I have 14 years old") and Irma read at the primer level in English at the beginning of the year. Irma felt especially uncomfortable as the oldest student in the fifth grade.

**Gilbert** (twelve), labeled learning disabled, also read at the primer level. He had a short attention span and had devised a number of creative work-avoidance strategies. His favorite pastime was raising doves.

**Rene** (eleven), definitely at odds with the system, belligerent, and a discipline problem, had spent much of his previous year in the principal's office. He read at the primer level.

**Apolinar** (ten), from Jalisco, Mexico ("in vacations we go to visit our grandfather in mexico"), where he had learned to read and write in Spanish, read at the 1.2 level. Apolinar was a partial breadwinner for his family: he worked, sometimes until 3:00 A.M., at his family's taco stand. He missed more days than any other student. Later, he would drop out an entire year to help in the family business.

Francisco (twelve), a shy child at the beginning of the year, read at the 1.2 level. His parents were also migrants. Francisco was one of eleven children, nine boys and two girls. He was born in Piedras Niegras, Mexico.

Alex, thirteen years old and painfully aware that he was three years older than most of the children, read at the 1.2 level. "I was born in Eagle Pass and I was born almost across the border and I was born in October 16 and my father was born in the same Dayet." (Eagle Pass, Texas, is separated from Piedras Negras, Mexico, only by the Rio Grande River.)

Florencia (twelve), a timid student in August, read at the 1.2 level. Later, she wrote, "I have a sister in law she is 15 years old and she has a baby girl her name is Beth and the Baby's name is Patty and I write her some Letters and she writes me some Letters too."

Christina (ten) was shy and reading three years below grade level (2.1). "I told [my sister] a secret and she told everybody that why I can not say any more secret. but anyway I still tell her about my secret. what are sister for that why I tell her all about my secret."

Roman (ten) returned from the fields late, in February, but managed to adapt to classroom procedures quickly. All members of his family were migrants. He often wrote about his experiences working in the fields. He read at the 2.1 level.

Patricia (eleven), from a large family of nine boys—one of whom was Francisco—and two girls, read at the 2.1 level at the beginning of the year. She wrote, "Sometimes we go to rivers and to parks and we also go to are parents house and we go to Black Rocks to see or sisters in law and are nieces and nephews and to see my two brothers that are their, with their wifes."

**Rosa** (age ten) was the busybody in the class, knowing everything and everybody, but was never a disturbance. She read at the 2.1 level. Her mother, a migrant, was divorced from her father, and Rosa lived with her father and step-mother.

**Monica** (ten) read at the 2.1 level. She seemed to be easily distracted and required more direction than any of the other students. When she worked, and kept on task, she performed.

**Lorenzo (Larry)** was also ten and a reluctant writer at first (see Chapter 3). He too read at the 2.1 level.

**Amy**, age ten, the daughter of migrants, returned to school in early November. She read at the 2.2 level. Her parents expressed their concern over her academic progress because of her unavoidably late arrival. She had never been retained but had come close in the past and was ever anxious.

**Jessica** (ten), a sensitive and self-conscious student, read at the 2.2 level. Jessica wrote, "My parents are nice I love them." She moved to Florida and completed her GED after the birth of her first child.

**Jaime**, a child of ten who loved football as well as other sports, read at the 2.2 level. He wrote, "I use to have five brothers but 1 died."

**Alejandra** (ten), the quietest, shiest girl in class, read at the 2.2 level. She later wrote, "I have one sister and two bothers and on vacations we go to corpus christi or some were else."

**Maria Anna** (ten) read at the 2.2 level. She wrote that she "was born in Jourdonton Tx and it is a french name I don't know aLot of it because when I was born I was so little."

**Lisa** was twelve; this was her second year in Robert's class. She had been retained the previous year because of her inability to attain the requisite scores in math. Lisa hated math and made no effort to improve. Robert felt guilty about retaining her but was forced to conform to district policy. During her previous year she had gained one year in reading proficiency, so she was now reading at level four. She was the daughter of poor, illiterate parents, who spent their weekends looking for aluminum cans along the major interstates or working in the fields. At the end of the year Lisa would be reading at the seventh-grade level.

These are the children of August whose writing we will display and attitudes we will discuss in the following chapters. Robert, himself bilingual, organized the class around reading and writing activities and expected results from every child. What these children needed, he believed, was not a teacher who would pity them for their lifestyles or for their poverty, but one who was sensitive and caring and confident enough to nudge them toward literacy. His classroom was a community. Teacher and students learned from each other. Failure at first remained uppermost in the students' minds, and while the fear of it decreased it never disappeared entirely. These fearful students eventually became learners, became exhilarated with their learning. During the course of the year, they began to anticipate and expect success. Their attendance rate of sixty-five percent the previous year increased to ninety-eight percent during their year together. The plan was to begin by sharing meaningful literacy events and written conversations in dialogue journals about *their* world. Robert began by learning about his students while reading them books as a demonstration of his own love of literacy. In so doing, he helped them to discover the magical encounters waiting for them in books.

# chapter
*Larry begins reluctantly*

*Many of us know firsthand
how politically motivated testing, grading,
and tracking policies have served to exclude
and punish those of us who did not understand
or wish to conform to education
that continues to subject us
to poverty and hopelessness.*

Sam Byrd, *Paper submitted for College of Education
course in Bilingual Education*

One morning in September Robert asked his students to write at least three lines, about any topic they chose. He collected their efforts and responded that evening. This marked the beginning of a written dialogue that continued throughout the school year.

When Robert read and responded to the journal entries, he neither criticized nor corrected them. Any errors (i.e., misspellings, mechanics, awkward syntax) he noted but left unmarked. He believed as does Donald Graves (1983) that "when errors are attended to in abundance, lo and behold, they come forth even more abundantly! What we pay attention to we reinforce" (314).

Miscues are generative, creative-constructing approximations that are communicative. However, to denote them as "errors" may imply that children had learned a rule and then forgotten it. While these students may have been taught rules in the past, they obviously did not learn them because the curriculum was not developmentally appropriate or "ethnosensitive" (Baugh 1980). Also, skills taught in isolation have no apparent logic or utility for the learner. We saw the students become more proficient in their individual journals through interlanguage (characterized by miscues) to arrive eventually at surface accuracy.

Attention to errors may indeed impede the development of writing skills. The danger is that

*when confronted with the numerous grammatical and mechanical [errors] that often characterize non-native English-speaking students' writing, many educators revert to extensive instruction in the basic low-order skills—an approach that can inhibit rather than enhance writing development. ("Interactive Writing" 1986, 19)*

Robert's directions were to attend to meaning rather than to mechanics and spelling. He believed that he needed to build the confidence of

# three

his students to write before he addressed the competence in writing. He encouraged his class to write in Spanish if they did not know the English or if they felt more comfortable with Spanish. Apolinar wrote in a mixture of both:

I like wreadin about flowers and people of all downs and I Like wreading in caset obout stories Like que Pequexo el mundo es and Like charly Brown and the book that you Read and gives quasten the book that ses Storistad must not die like la vibora ingrata and ▨ cabayo iLa avispa DoDas es libros me gustan amy. ▨

Oh ▨ I like Reading about MoASters too.

*I like reading about flowers and about people of all towns and I like reading with the cassette about stories like "How Small the World Is" and like Charlie Brown and the book that you read that asks questions—the book that's called Stories That Must Not Die, like "The Ungrateful Snake" and "The Horse and the Bee." I like all of these books. Oh, I like reading and monsters too.*

We do not wish to discount or ignore the errors that appeared in student journals—the students made many, especially during the first part of the semester. Robert considered the errors signs of their willingness to write, and therefore progress. He would attend to the errors later; for now he wanted only that these children risk putting their words down on paper. Since they were very concerned with errors, he told them that if they didn't make mistakes they wouldn't learn as well or as quickly.

However hesitant they were initially, most of the class did write entries. *Larry began reluctantly!* He was terrified. He handed in a blank piece of paper; Robert responded, "How can I answer you if you don't write to me?" and then asked, "Does anything bother you about writing?"

Larry answered:

*Well I can't spell right. That's what bothers me about writing.*

Larry's reaction was symptomatic. For the first few days, the students asked: "Do we only have to write three lines?" a normal inquiry from children who view writing as a distasteful activity to be endured and gotten through. Three lines were all that were required; and most students wrote only three lines.

The entries gradually lengthened once the students were into the routine of writing. They wrote about what they were learning or found interesting as well as about their lives—the daily occurrences that would have been missed except that they wrote about them in their journals. Children who were not fluent, or were nonwriters, or were reluctant (like Larry) became more fluent, less tentative.

Journal writing appeared to be developmental. From a few words in a few sentences, the children began to write more than the required minimum. Occasionally it was difficult to understand meanings (sometimes poor handwriting contributed). One of the early entries Robert received is shown in Figure 3–1; it is understandable, but only with much effort. If there were difficulties in discerning meaning, Robert and the writer conferred to clarify.

Gradually, with more practice, and with Robert's concise responses written in clear handwriting, the children's entries began to improve in quality and quantity. Their confidence improved as the fear of writing, of putting something down on paper, diminished; they began to write. Robert's responses to their entries provided a demonstration and

**figure 3–1**

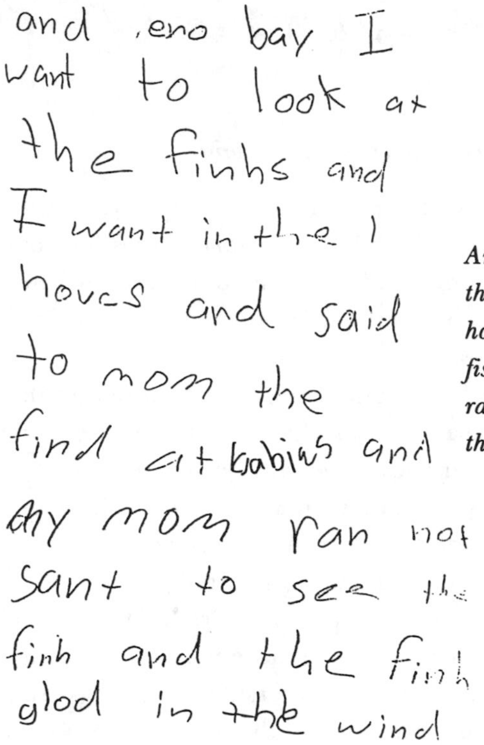

and ,eno bay I
want to look at
the finhs and
I want in the l
houes and said
to mom the
find at babins and
my mom ran not
sant to see the
finh and the finh
glod in the wind

*And one day I went to look at
the fishes and I went in the
house and said to mom the
fish had babies and my mom
ran outside to see the fish and
the fish glowed in the wind*

model of standard, written English. Even though he did not correct, he did, as opportunity arose in responses, correctly spell or restate with correct structure the words they had misspelled or misstated. If they did not know a word, or had difficulty in understanding a response, he encouraged them to ask him or a classmate. If they were unsure of spelling, Robert would give the first three letters of the word and have them look it up in the dictionary. They would then place the word in their word bank, their own dictionary, which they kept in their writing folder.

During a later stage, when their entries were longer (sometimes two or more pages), trust grew where it had formerly been absent and the students wrote without the sword of possible failure over their heads. They could not fail journal writing. They began to like and value reading and writing and ultimately learning itself. They had discovered the utility of literacy.

## The purpose of journals

What did the children write about? What did writing in a journal do for them? Did their writing become better? Did their errors decrease as they became fluent? Did they think better? Did writing in the expressive mode translate into writing in the transactional or academic mode? We could see some, but not all, of the answers in their journals.

Writing in the journals put an end to doubts about being *able* to write. The students became more confident as they became more proficient. In their journals the children could also accomplish a number of specific tasks. They wrote about what they were learning; they wrote about their lives and their homes; they wrote about classroom events; mainly they wrote about themselves.

### SHARING

Cummins (1986, 26; 1989, 1994; McCaleb 1994) writes that when parents are accepted by the school, by the teacher, as partners in the educational process, they become more interested in having their children do well. They are able to monitor their children's progress; they tend to ask about school, about assignments. Their interest is a form of encouragement. Parents can lend an extremely supportive role in learning. Parents can help encourage progress in reading by having their children read to them at home. Children who read to their parents make more progress than children who do not. Our children's parents became enthusiastic partners.

Robert encouraged the children to take books home to read and share not only with their parents but with their siblings as well.

Jessica writes in her journal about reading stories to her younger brother:

*I like to read to my baby brother stories about green and ham and he loves to hear it.*

*I like to read to my baby brother stories about greens and ham, and he loves to hear it.*

Robert responds, "You are doing great. Keep reading to your brother." Jessica later writes:

*And I want to tell you thank you.*

*And I want to tell you thank you.*

Robert asks, "What are you thanking me for?" Jessica responds:

*For the idea of reading a lot and letting me take books home. I enjoy writing book. My best book is the state, Because there's more pages on it.*

*For the idea of reading a lot and letting me take books home. I enjoy writing books. My best book is the [one on the] states, because there's more pages in it.*

Norma writes about helping her younger brother learn how to read:

> well yesterday I help to him in math + words
> in English I have some books + yesterday
> I help brother in math and words in English
> I Like help us because I like teacher and
> is beautiful for me yesterday

*Well yesterday I helped him in math and in English words. I have some books and yesterday I helped my brother in math and in English words. I like helping because I like [being a] teacher. It was beautiful for me yesterday.*

Francisco tells about the difficulty his brother, monolingual in Spanish, is experiencing in learning to read and his parent's concern:

> mad with him because he didn't. not my mother want to get read
> + do math or time tables. he just want to
> play with some body Like me or Alfonso

*My mother got mad at him because he didn't want to read and do math or times tables. He just wanted to play with somebody, like me or Alfonso.*

Robert responds by agreeing that he is also concerned about Francisco's brother's future if he doesn't learn how to read. Francisco answers:

*I thihek that he know how to read bout he didn't not want to read a book and h; no how to write in Spanish bout he didn't not want to writing aro no why he didn't not want to read and writing, We have alots of books over there boutt he didn't not wan to read that books*

*I think that he knows how to read but he didn't want to read a book. He knows how to write in Spanish but he didn't want to write. I don't know why he didn't want to read and write. We have lots of books over there but he didn't want to read those books.*

**Robert encourages Francisco by offering some strategies. Francisco agrees:**

*I can take the book today and read at home to my brother and my mom too*

*I can take the book today and read at home to my brother and my mom too.*

Florencia writes:

I'm Reading to my
other cousin, And yesturday
I Read them a story of the
three Little bears, And they
Like them,

*I'm reading to my other cousins. And yesterday I read them a story of the three little bears. And they liked them.*

She also writes about reading to her parents during vacation:

I had a nice vacation And I
Read A book to my mom & dad And
my moom said she Liked it And
dad said he Likes it too.

*I had a nice vacation. I read a book to my mom and dad, and my mom said she liked it and my dad said he liked it too.*

By encouraging the children to take books home to read and to share, Robert was attempting to replicate a literacy event, to spread and extend the boundaries of their education, to involve the home as a place where learning continues. Sharing reading experiences with others and reading aloud helps children to learn to read; when children read to their younger siblings and cousins, and to their parents, literacy becomes an event in their homes.

Robert found that parents were beginning to "pick up on" reading by being read to by their children. As Florencia writes:

I'm Reading the new books
you braut And I Like
them And I'm going
to take one home so
I can Read on to my
Dad And mom.

*I'm reading the new books you brought. I like them, and I'm going to take one home so I can read it to my dad and mom.*

### ACCESS

Dialogue promotes learning because the journals provide students personal and direct access to their teacher. How many times has a teacher, while helping one child, been unaware that other children need help? The journals provide a place where children can seek help, can inquire, and can request clarification; the teacher in turn can inquire about their work, their progress, their feelings. In one study, Shuy (1987a) reports that students who write in dialogue journals more than double the number of questions they ask their teacher. Teachers, during the course of a normal school day, cannot hope to respond to all their children's questions, but they can more easily answer questions that appear in journals. The dialogue journal becomes not only an avenue of access but also a forum for personalized, developmentally appropriate teaching. Teacher access is very evident in the children's exchanges with Robert.

Jessica inquires:

*You tell us to write a lot and why do you write a little bit.*

*Why do you tell us to write a lot and you write a little bit?*

Robert responds, "You have to remember that I write answers in twenty-two journals every day. Do you still think I don't write a lot?"

On another occasion, Norma worries about her lack of English skills:

*because I don't no much words and ingles because this year I want learn the ingles. I no I need more words because I need much & much ingles because much of teachers she's know the ingles & no spanish I need more Ingles because I want talk with what ever the teacher.*

*I know I need [to know] more words because I don't know many words in English. This year I want to learn English. I need much more English because many teachers know English but not Spanish. I need more English because I want to talk with whatever the teacher [I have].*

Robert responds:

*Next year in sixth grade many of your teachers will not know Spanish, so you are right: you will need to know much more English. The more you read and write in English the better you will know it. What words can I help you with?*

Norma takes this suggestion and begins to read more books; but when looking for the newer ones, she can't find them. Robert says he has taken them to the university for sharing but will return them to the classroom shortly. Norma acknowledges that this is okay and then asks,

How many teachers do you have? Do you like the university?

*How many teachers do you have? Do you like the university?*

Robert assures her that he does.

Patricia asks a question in her journal that may have been inappropriate for her to ask in class:

Why my Science Report is not in the window?

*Why is my science report not in the window?*

Robert tells her, "I only put a few reports in the window because I want to have them ready to laminate tomorrow."

Later, toward the end of the year, Patricia, growing in confidence, asks:

Can I write you Just one time in spanish in the Journl?

*Can I write you just one time in Spanish in the Journal?*

Robert replies, "If you want you can write to me in Spanish in the journal. I enjoy reading and writing in Spanish, too!" So Patricia begins:

Bueno te Voy a escibrir. en Espacñol.

*Bueno te voy a Escibrir en Espanol.*

Robert responds in Spanish. The crucial point is that Patricia is becoming more proficient in English, and at the same time she has an excellent chance of becoming proficient in her first language. Patricia values using and maintaining her primary language and has the insight to ask for input in Spanish and practice time in reading and writing Spanish. She is now developing Spanish and her second language concurrently. She is becoming biliterate.

Francisco, ill with the flu, continues to write in his journal, asking his sister, Patricia, who is in the same class, to take his journal to school. While Francisco has been ill, the class has begun a social science project. Each student has chosen a letter and found a country beginning with that letter to write a report on. Worried, Francisco writes:

Mr. B, did they pick a Letter for the countries teacher I pick Letter E because the countries is cuetador and when did pick a Letter or a countries. Bout get Letter E for me for the countries

*Mr. B, did they pick a letter for the countries? Teacher, I pick letter* C *because the country [I want to write about] is Cuetador. When [they] pick a letter of a country, get letter* C *for me for the countries.*

Robert responds that *C* has already been selected:

*Francisco, I'm sorry but Alex already took the* C *to do China. I have reserved the letter* A *for you to do. This will be the first page in our book so I wanted to give it to my best worker,* YOU!

Apolinar suggests some changes in class routine:

wy don't you let us
have a fry Time like in 2:30 like thad Mr. im Reding

*Why don't you let us have free time at 2:30, like that Mr. I'm reading [about].*

Apolinar likes to write and he especially likes to combine writing with art. He tells why and then suggests a dedication for a future book:

Because we Draw.
at the paper and write on it all the time
on I like to Do art in apaper Because I like to DO
Art a lot.

*Because we draw on the paper and write on it all the time. I like to do art on a paper because I like to do art a lot.*

Mr. Bahruth coold we dede

cate the next book
to Miss new Somm

*Could we dedicate the next book to Miss Newsomm?*

   Florencia inquires:

. If Some one helps me with
my homework wood you get
mad.

*If someone helps me with my homework, would you get mad?*

Florencia also expresses her anxiety concerning putting math
problems on the board:

I like to do
division problems. But when I'm
in front doing wone I get
nerves.

*I like to do division problems. But when I'm in front doing one I get nervous.*

Robert replies, "I won't get mad if someone helps you. I let Norma
and Irma help, don't I? [And] you shouldn't get nervous, because we
are all your friends here." Yet Florencia persists:

> But iknow I
> nave my hair cut And I'm more embrr:
> And some times I get more nervoa
> when I think thatethe problem is
> ifong.

*But now I have my hair cut and I'm more embarrassed. Sometimes, I get more nervous when I think that the problem is wrong.*

Robert asks her whether she is still studying her times tables at home. Florencia answers:

> Im studing my times tables athome
> And I'm going To fricy harder in
> math.

*I'm studying my times tables at home and I'm going to try harder in math.*

Amy, an anxious child, has a number of observations, including her desire to succeed:

> how am I doing
> in math    am I going to pass to th 6th grade .

*How am I doing in math? Am I going to pass to the 6th grade?*

*Mr. Bahruth am I on your List from Staing in 5th grade? Plese tell me!*

*Mr. Bahruth am I on your list for staying in 5th grade? Please tell me!*

*not Like writhings in my Iournal Becguse I do not Know what to writh in it*

*I do not like writing in my journal because I do not know what to write in it.*

And a request:

*can you read us a book about Charlottes Wed on Monday Charlottes wed is a good book ther are 22 chapters and it was writhen by E.B white and Authoor. Stuart Little. and Pictures by. Garth Willams*

*Can you read us a book about Charlotte's Web on Monday? Charlotte's Web is a good book. There are 22 chapters and it was written by E.B. White and the author Stuart Little, with pictures by Garth Williams.*

Larry, as we have seen, was reluctant to write. But once into it, he became an enthusiastic journalist. He asks,

> Have you play football
> weirnd you were little with anther kids

*Have you played football when you were little with other kids?*

The conversation involved football up to and including the Super Bowl. Larry also asks for help:

> OK how about putting a few problems of
> divison or times.

*How about putting a few problems of division or multiplication [in my journal]?*

And Robert does.

**LEARNING**

The students wrote about what they were learning, about books they had either heard Robert read or had read themselves. The journal, a repository of mostly expressive writing, contained transactional writing as well. Book reports have been used extensively in the past to measure writing skill and the depth of understanding that a student takes away from a book. Traditionally, students could write about plot and characters. Figure 3–2 is Larry's book report on the basal that the class had been reading. Larry's report has an introduction, a discussion of plot, and a conclusion.

figure 3–2

I like to read because I can move to other book like
I was in curbstone Dragon and I move the book
Mustard Seed magic.

Do you enjoy the stories in those books or are there
other books you enjoy more? You have to read these books
because they will help you to be able to read any book you
want to later on.

The storie I like in all of the stories of all
the one I like was the Mystery of the
Moving snowman if I read all the stories in
Mustard seed magic maybe I can pick a other
Storie that can be more good then the storie
of the mystery of the moving snowman. But
this Book is the best of all the books I ever
read in my hole years. Because I like the
storie of the mystery of the moving snowman
because who a boy or a girl find how the
Snowman movid to house and house,
How ever knowes th anwer wines a
sled, And a boy and a girl saw the snow
snowman on there yard. They were
working together and they win the
sled. Thates why I like that storie and
I thing thates the stonie I like Best
of all the storeies I ever read in all
the book I ever read in all my
yeares is mustaRd seed magic.

The story I like of all the stories was the Mystery of the Moving Snowman. If I read all the stories in Mustard Seed Magic maybe I can pick another story that is better than the Mystery of the Moving Snowman. But this is the best of all the stories I have ever read in my life. Because I like the story of the Mystery of the Moving Snowman because if a boy or a girl find out how the snowman moved from house to house, whoever knows the answer wins a sled. And a boy and a girl saw the snowman in their yard. They were working together and they won the sled. That's why I like the story and I think that's the story I like best of all the stories I ever read in the book and I have ever read in my whole life is Mustard Seed Magic.

Discussions of an academic nature continued. Toward the end of the year, Robert asks Amy, "How do you feel about writing now?" She responds:

> I feel fine writing Books.
> How do you feel writing Books?
> It is easier now. Because
> it stated hard and it is
> easer now.
> I like doing both things
> writing Books and writing in my
> Journal. Because it showed
> me
> how to spell.

*I feel fine writing books. How do you feel writing books? It is easier now. Because it started hard and it is easier now. I like doing both things, writing books and writing in my journal, because it showed me how to spell.*

Florencia also had many problems with spelling but feels that she finally is learning:

> Remember when I
> didn't know how to spell
> studyin now I now how to

*Remember when I didn't know how to spell studying? Now I know how to.*

Francisco also writes transactionally, but about kinds of books that interest him:

I like to read book about my teacher read to us. My teacher reads books. I like to Read books about animls and people I like to read books off animls because they toumy about dogs and Elephant and oh cands of animls. And I like to read books of people because they meyctimee lough / because they make people lough

*I like to read books like the ones my teacher reads to us. My teacher reads books. I like to read books about animals and people. I like to read books about animals because they tell me about dogs and elephants and all kinds of animals. And I like to read books about people because they make me laugh, because they make people laugh.*

## ASPIRATIONS

As these children continued to read, write, and learn, their aspirations tended to change and their expectations of themselves became more demanding. It is almost as though they knew that education, the ability to read and write, provided access to more options with more attractive and wider possibilities and alternatives. Throughout the year, they discussed their aspirations, their goals, their prospects with Robert. As they wrote they thought about what they wanted to do. In March, toward the end of the year, they wrote essays for a book they entitled *Great Expectations*. But before writing about their expectations, they explored some of their choices in their journals.

Jessica wrote,

I want to go to college. Mr. Bahruth how many years does it take to go to college does it take until you finish high school then they send you to college. I never want to flunck because if I flunck I feel bad. That's why I'm study hard and do my work. My mom said to study hard

I want to go to a school that teach me how to take care of people. I want to be a good person that takes care of all people. I told my mom she didn't say anything.

*I want to go to college. Mr. Bahruth, how many years does it take to go to college? Does it take until you finish high school, then they send you to college? I never want to flunk, because if I flunk I feel bad. That's why I study hard and do my work. My mom said to study hard.*

*I want to go to a school that teaches me how to take care of people. I want to be a good person that takes care of all people. I told my mom. She didn't say anything.*

Norma discussed her future with her parents:

I talk with my mother + father + my mother said, mr. Bahruth said you paint pretty why you don't study for painter + I said I want to study for teacher + she said ok. what ever you want that's fine O.K.

*I talked with my mother and father, and my mother said, "Mr. Bahruth said you paint pretty. Why don't you study to be a painter?" I said, "I want to study to be a teacher." She said, "O.K. Whatever you want, that's fine. O.K."*

Francisco writes:

*I told my mother that when I grow up I want to be a computer [programmer] or a doctor. What do you need to do to be a computer worker? To be a computer worker you need to go to college.*

## Key notions

Successful learners take risks. Asher (1985) says, "If students feel comfortable and secure, then they can learn." These children had been neither comfortable nor secure. They had a mental block evidenced in their behavior, a lack of confidence and motivation. They were anxious. They had a set of negative attitudes toward school, learning, and teachers. They were preoccupied with the possibility of failure.

No one could fail the dialogue journal! Robert was interested in growth and fluency, in talking with his students. When they discovered they would not be "hammered" (as one student called corrections marked on papers), they moved from considering the dialogue journal merely an exercise they had to get through each morning to considering it a way of talking with writing. Just when during the course of the year this change actually occurred is not clear; it happened gradually and at different times for each child. Growth in writing development is erratic, but growth in confidence is not. Their confidence rose when they became so involved in writing and reading that they forgot they were reading or writing a language they had not mastered. As they became successful journal writers, their self-respect grew. It was as if they had experienced a long losing season and suddenly, quite unexpectedly, they had begun to win. The change in attitude was enormous. We shall see further evidence of this change in the chapters that follow.

## Observations

There are a number of observations we can make that point to the positive effects of daily journal entries. English-language proficiency and fluency increased; handwriting, punctuation, and spelling improved.

The students acquired correct spelling when they deemed it important for their writing. Many invented spellings when they did not know how to spell a word. *Motorcycle* was spelled *modrsikel* in Alex's journal. (He eventually learned to spell it correctly.) Among some of the other invented spellings: *dedecate, hungred, brekfast, mountans, starded, egle, wone, child* (palatalized from *killed*), *yesturday, alians, divaided, picans, bacasion.*

Several students generalized spelling rules; one such spelling rule was the silent *e* that occurs in words such as *bide, hide, cane.* This *e* also appeared in their journals on words such as *looke, cousine, agene, hande, abaute, hite, fare, thate, schoole, ate, sede* (*said*), *pene.*

As students read Robert's responses incorporating the correct spellings, their spelling became more accurate. In the process of acquiring spelling ability, a student might spell a word correctly and incorrectly in the same passage. Variation, in any of its aspects, is typical of language acquisition (Beebe 1988). Some students insisted that Robert correct their spelling. He asked them to circle words they were unsure of, and he used those words in his responses. Spelling also tended to become more accurate when the children began to publish and edit what they had written (see the following chapters).

Above all, the dialogue journal is a sharing enterprise. The journals revealed many facets of their lives. Robert learned of the difficulties they were encountering in their school work as well as their everyday problems. They felt free to ask their teacher to share his life—"wind" he was a kid. They questioned: "How am I doing?" They asserted: "I want to go to college." They grieved: "My brother died." Florencia wrote,

I LiKe Roing more in my Journal
Because we can talk together +
you can now ABaute my Life
+I can now ABaute your Life

*I like writing more in my journal because we can talk together. You can know about my life and I can know about your life.*

Reading and responding to dialogue journals tends, we suggest, to humanize teachers and make them more aware of and accessible to their students' lives, both in and out of the classroom. The dialogue journal is also a bridge, a springboard to transactional, academic writing. Some children anticipated academic writing by writing about what they were learning. They wrote, became readers, and then wrote again (Calkins 1986). We could judge the level of their competence and their growth by looking at their journals. They also learned to look through some of their earlier entries and compare them with their later ones. Their growth was enormous, and they were aware of that growth.

Attitudes toward writing, reading, and learning changed. Larry, initially a reluctant writer, writes later in the semester:

*do you remember the frist day I didn't write guess like one line, I like writeing in my Journal*

*Do you remember the first day I didn't write just like one line? I like writing in my journal.*

Their entries were in folders, and they drew designs or pictures on the front covers. Larry asks permission to begin a second journal because he has run out of pages in his first, "but this time," he says, "I will make the cover of the journal pretty, not like this journal." His first cover, Figure 3–3, is highly tentative, incorporates small figures, faintly drawn, with little color, an "okay, if you want a cover, here it is" cover. The second cover, Figure 3–4, reflects his interest, his change of attitude, an exuberance missing from the first.

figure 3–3

figure 3–4

Writing began with the dialogue journal, reading began with extensive opportunities to hear stories read aloud and to read self-selected books silently. When Robert first requested that his students write to him daily, they were wary ("Are you going to grade?"), but they soon realized that by writing they also received Robert's responses. The journal was an ideal forum. By focusing on their areas of interest (they chose the topic), Robert could respond to their entries with language that each could understand. His written responses, tailored individually for each child, provided a daily reading lesson. Children were writers one minute, readers the next (Calkins 1986; Hansen 1987).

## In summary

Robert explored various types of journals before settling on the dialogue journal. Each type has a different purpose, a different focus. A journal can, for example, be either public or private. Public journals can be shared with others, with classmates. A private journal may be reviewed and consulted by the student only; or it may have a restrictive readership, read by the teacher only. Robert was the audience for his students' dialogue journals. It is not important where students write, or what they write about. What is important is that they write every day. The strength of journal writing resides in the children's writing regularly "about what is alive and vital and real for them—and their writing becomes the curriculum" (Calkins 1986, 8).

Dan Kirby and Tom Liner (1988) point out that the journal is

*one of those phenomena of English teaching: an instant hit with teachers everywhere. It zoomed like a skyrocket through every cookbook and*

*conference. . . . Seven million teachers did it to their kids on Monday. Some*
*teachers swear by it; some swear at it. Some do both. (57)*

Journal advocates have been known to ask their students to write in
their journals on any subject or area of interest to them or on school
subjects only. Robert's students wrote on any topic. There is latitude
in the kind of response. Teachers may, for example, correct their
students' entries. Robert chose not to, except indirectly. Teachers may
not respond in writing at all. Robert always responded. Where entries
are written may also vary. Students may write in class, or they may
write at home, or they may write at home and in class. Robert
provided time each morning for students to write their entries.
Students may write in their journals daily, or they may not. Robert's
students wrote daily. Robert's main purpose in choosing a daily
journal was to provide a place for the children to engage in "nonrisk"
writing, to remove fear, reduce anxieties, and increase fluency, to
nurture the ability to write more than a few perfunctory sentences.
Robert wanted to show them that they could indeed write.

The dialogue journal was a *catalytic converter*. It helped transform
reluctant writers and learners into successful and eager students—
students who convinced themselves that they could learn. The
dialogue journal is not a panacea to cure all writing ills. Fulwiler
(1987) points out that writing in a journal won't change students
overnight; it won't take uninterested students and miraculously turn
them into active learners. What it does is make it more difficult for
students to remain uninterested and inactive. The journal entries of
Robert's students eventually increased in length, and spelling as well
as punctuation became more standard, although not perfect. Time
spent responding also increased. At the beginning of the year it took

Robert approximately twenty minutes to write his responses to the relatively short entries. Toward the end of the year, as entries increased in length, the responses took much longer.

To increase confidence and self-esteem; to turn failure into success; to promote positive attitudes; and to convert reluctant, hesitant learners into enthusiastic and motivated students—these were the goals. Robert and his students found that the dialogue journal provided a safe and protected harbor for reading and writing, for overall language development, and for building the confidence that all successful learners must have. By encouraging the writing of journals and by writing responses, Robert not only gave the children a forum in which to write without risk but he also demonstrated the importance and joy of reading and writing in his own life. The journey to increased literacy had begun.

While the dialogue journal became a forum for expressing anxieties and other concerns, it also became a forum out of which future assignments and topics could emerge and grow. It is to these that we now turn.

# chapter

## *Christina finds play in writing*

*. . . one can hypothesize that writing is something that everyone ought to be able to do and enjoy, as naturally as singing, dancing, or play. Like singing, dancing, and play, writing may be one of those activities that all children enjoy—and enjoy learning to do better—until, all too often, they become discouraged or disinterested because something happens to inhibit their free and natural expression. And that something that happens can often be associated with education or training; it results in a loss of spontaneity, a painful self-consciousness of 'error,' a reluctance to perform and learn because of a perceived inability to achieve certain extrinsic standards.*

Frank Smith, *Demonstrations, Engagement and Sensitivity: A Revised Approach to Language Learning*

Writing can be rewarding. We have seen that the dialogue journal helped convince Robert's students that they could write as it helped increase their feelings of adequacy. To reduce any remaining apprehension, he devised a number of activities to encourage the class to write and share their work with their classmates. They desperately needed assignments that would enable them to succeed. Our chapter describes activities that, while demanding, were things the children could do successfully.

*Play* is not usually associated with writing; yet Robert wanted writing to seem playful, something the children would want to do and look forward to doing, as well as risk doing. Children usually succeed at play. They learn to play games, some of which are extremely complex and time-consuming. They learn to play because play is social and satisfying. Language is also social and satisfying, in addition to being creative and challenging. Robert wanted writing to be like play: social, satisfying, and rewarding—but especially fun. "Playing with language," the Nilsens (1978) say, "is inherent in humans" (129).

Gaining the cooperation and sparking the interest of children not accustomed to spending a large part of their school day writing and reading was Robert's aim. Reluctant children needed to learn that they could write. A completed assignment was that success. Christina, a child who did not like to write, learned through the year that writing was satisfying, rewarding, and fun. In her poem she describes the joy of living on a farm:

*Im going to say a little poem.*
*It is about a farm.*
*It has bugs and a tree and three butterflies and 2 flowers and a burro and a*
*camel and 2 tractors and a banana tree and a house.*

# four

*I like to live on a farm because it is fun.*
*You would have a lot of room, and you can play and you can go hunting.*
*That is fun to do.*
*We can cook outside.*
*And we can go fishing.*

## Publication

Class-published books were an adventure, a source of play and motivation. The communal act of publishing their own essays increased the students' interest in writing. It was not difficult to enlist the participation of Christina and her classmates to write for publication. It was a new and rewarding experience. Publication served to widen the audience for essays to include classmates and parents. The students took their books home to show and read to parents, who were able to acknowledge what their child and Robert were writing. While the children and Robert did not publish everything they wrote, they always wrote with publication in mind. Publication gave the class impetus; the children learned that they did not write solely to a teacher.

Publication was an instant hit because it was a social activity. Following Graves's (1983) example, the class published extensively and included the following elements in each book:

A laminated, illustrated cover.
A title page.
A table of contents.
A dedication page (one text was dedicated to Donald Graves, "who showed us how").

Books were subsequently bound with a spiral provided by friends in the school district. While the dialogue journals were private written conversations between the children and Mr. B., the books were public. They were shared with other classes, with the principal, with families, and with teachers. Books provided the children an opportunity to compare their proficiency with the proficiency of their classmates as well as an avenue for expressing their individuality at their own level of interest and ability. A book demonstrated what the class could do cooperatively. It was a model of where the class stood in the development of its writing ability at any one time.

Having the children write drafts of their papers allowed revision and editing to find their place. Revision became important, as shown by students' increased interest in rewriting and "making meaning," to get what they had to say just right. Just as the children washed their hands and faces, combed their hair, and wore their best clothes for the class picture, so too they made sure that what they published was as free from blemishes, such as misspelled words, as possible. Even so, errors did not disappear or diminish overnight. Children were overheard pointing out to classmates their misspellings. For children who write for publication editing becomes a crucial skill. The class picture is public and permanent. So are books. Robert did not have to urge his students to revise or edit.

The essays were not critiqued or edited once they were published; however, students received suggestions from classmates and Robert before handing them in. The children were writers, members of what Smith (1988) calls the *literacy club,* a club that holds there is little difference between published authors and themselves. Writers write and publish. Period! They did the same.

A strong sense of ownership pervaded the children's writing. In

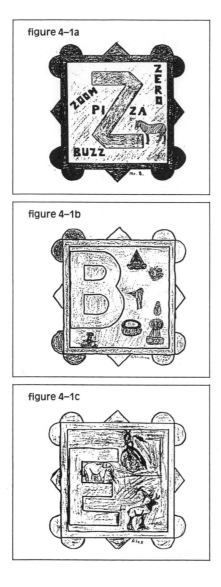

figure 4–1a

figure 4–1b

figure 4–1c

traditional classes, if the children were required to write at all, their teacher would assign a topic, the children would write, and the papers would be collected, corrected, and returned. In this class, the responsibility for writing was shared with their classmates. If they did not write and edit well, not only would their book suffer but so would their reputations for being careful and tidy with their writing.

## The first book!

The class was excited and looking forward to publishing a book containing their individual efforts! The first book contained drawings of each letter of the alphabet. This assignment may seem elementary, especially for a fifth-grade class, but for students who had little experience in making letters or working with the alphabet or even with alphabetical order, it was ideal. Robert provided each child with a square form for the letter, and drew and illustrated the letter *Z* (shown in Figure 4–1a) as a model. Then the children designed their own letters. They could color; they could include pictures as well as words to illustrate their letter.

The children talked about the alphabet as they drew. After the drawings were completed, Robert had the children stand in alphabetical order according to their letter and pronounce both the name of the letter and words beginning with the letter. It was an activity to increase their awareness and understanding of the relationships between letters and sounds, to increase their sensitivity to standardized spelling, and to increase their confidence that they could make a standard form for each letter.

Christina drew the letter *B*, along with objects beginning with *B* (Figure 4–1b). Alex included pictures of animals (Figure 4–1c), as did

Larry, along with the brand name *Lee* (Figure 4–1d). Norma spelled words beginning with *O* (Figure 4–1e); Gilbert drew *Y* (Figure 4–1f).

Putting the letters in alphabetical order, in a book, demonstrated to the class that their efforts were worthy. The children asked to take the book home. A checkout card was placed on the inside back cover, and throughout the semester the letter book, entitled *Abecedario*, as well as the other subsequently published books, could be checked out and shared at home.

What did this act of designing a letter do for the children? First, it was interesting and motivating. It taught or clarified alphabetical order and helped the children find words in the dictionary. It called on the children's ability to design and add figures and color. Even though some children were better at designing and drawing than others, all succeeded in drawing and illustrating a letter and sharing what they had drawn.

The skills of revising and editing are important but are not easily taught or learned. Children want the first draft to be their final draft (Urzua 1987, 285). Publishing made it necessary for the students to revise and edit. When asked to share their drawings of letters, some, after seeing their classmates' efforts, wanted to revise and edit. They learned they did not have to be right the first or even the third or fourth time. There was time for revision and redrafting—skills that were carried over to their essays. Time to share and compare led to better manuscripts.

## Writing with the rebus

The children were obsessed with spelling accurately. They were always asking, "How to do you spell ———?" This focus on correct

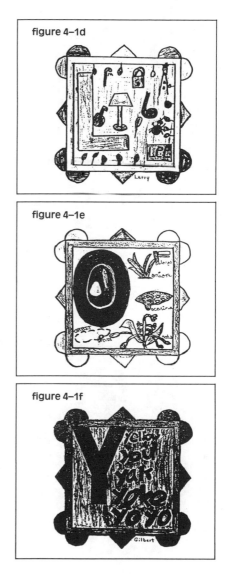

figure 4–1d

figure 4–1e

figure 4–1f

spelling was not strange or unusual, because they were accustomed to being graded on spelling and mechanics. It is no wonder they were concerned with spelling and mechanics, even while they were writing their first drafts.

In order to free his time to listen to and comment on their drafts, Robert asked students either to circle the words they were not sure of or to spell them as they sounded—even to draw a word if necessary. The attitude Robert demonstrated was, "Don't worry about spelling while you are writing; there is plenty of time to take care of words you misspelled later."

The children used all three techniques in their manuscripts—not only circling words or providing an approximate phonetic script but also representing pictorially those that lent themselves to the use of the rebus.

This methodology led to a book written with the rebus. The students entitled it *Love Letters* (the book's cover is shown in Figure 4–2a). Three "Dear Mom" letters—Christina's, Lisa's, and Apolinar's —are reproduced in Figures 4–2b through 4–2d.

Writing *Love Letters* was a fun, nonthreatening activity. The rebus was employed for words they didn't know how to spell, but also for words they *did* know how to spell. No one had to ask, "How do you draw ———?" Children compared drawings and asked for advice from Mr. B and their classmates before writing a final draft. The order in which to present the papers was agreed on, a table of contents prepared, a cover designed, and the book published.

Several days later, Robert asked the children to look at their papers and circle the words they needed to learn to spell. They compiled lists of words, organized them in alphabetical order, attempted to locate them in the dictionary and, failing that, asked a classmate or Robert

figure 4–2a

figure 4–2b

for help, and finally wrote them on the board spelled correctly, accompanied by a short definition. Since the students were anxious about spelling correctly, Robert used the list as a spelling list, and gave a spelling test at the end of the week. Spelling took on a real-world experience in their work, and scores on spelling tests improved.

figure 4–2c

mom,

I watered the 🌸 🌸 'sand the 🌳 's
and I washed the ◎ ⓘ's for you.
after that I cleaned the 🏠's and
washed ⊚ ⓘ's for you when you were
gone. Then we went to the 🏪. Then we
went home to wait for the 📬. after
we went the 🚗 wash. I washed the
both 🚙 🚗's. 💗, LISA

figure 4–2d

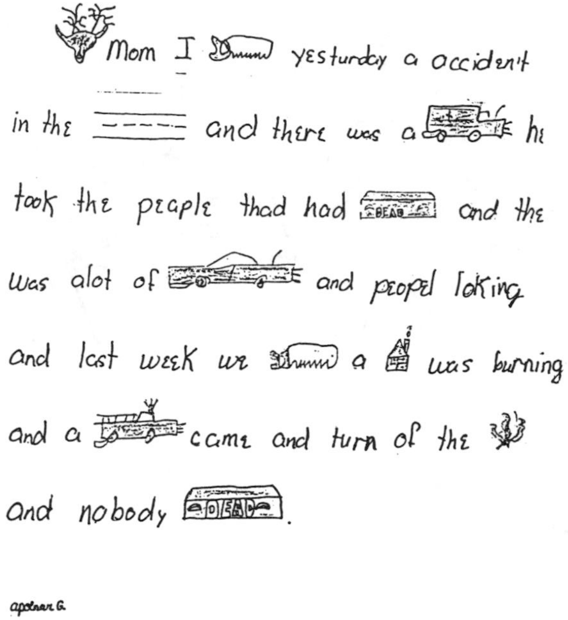

Mom I 🐷 yesturday a occident
in the ═══ and there was a 🚙 hi
took the peaple thad had 🚗 and the
was alot of 🚗 and peopel loking
and last week we 🐷 a 🏠 was burning
and a 🚒 came and turn of the 🔥
and nobody 🚌.

*apetaar G.*

The activity of using their writing for spelling quizzes continued throughout the year. By reducing any pressure for being perfect on a first draft, by providing time for writing each day, and by taking care of spelling and mechanics at the proper stage, Robert encouraged writers to look forward to writing.

## Conversation pieces

Children love to talk and they love verbal play. Robert encouraged an attitude of "yes, talking" (Enright and McCloskey 1988) in his classroom while students worked on projects. It was not a silent class but one full of conversation. An additional rule, "Respect the rights of others," decreased the time that Robert had to spend attending to matters of discipline as the children became aware there was a time for working and a time to let their classmates work. They learned the discourse of the classroom and began to see the differences between natural language and speech written down.

At this grade level, students were just getting into abstract punctuation, such as direct and indirect spoken discourse. The workbook assigned by the district consisted of a set of punctuation rules along with a number of sentences for the students to punctuate. Robert decided to combine the children's verbal play with the editing rules for punctuating direct speech. He made up his own punctuation exercises using pairs of students who transcribed conversations they had with each other.

Mr. B. paired himself with Gilbert, with Gilbert portraying a customer calling the Pizza Hut to place an order (their transcribed conversation is shown in Figure 4–3a). Gilbert began by "talking" in complete sentences, but halfway through he assumed a more conversational style, with the ellipsis of information already known to both interlocutors. From Gilbert's "I want to order a medium pizza" to his "Dr. Pepper" (in answer to the query, "What would you like to drink?"), the conversation evolved toward more authentic discourse. Punctuation marks were added and used correctly, as were other editing skills.

Christina and Maria Anna paired themselves as a city employee and

---

**figure 4–3a**

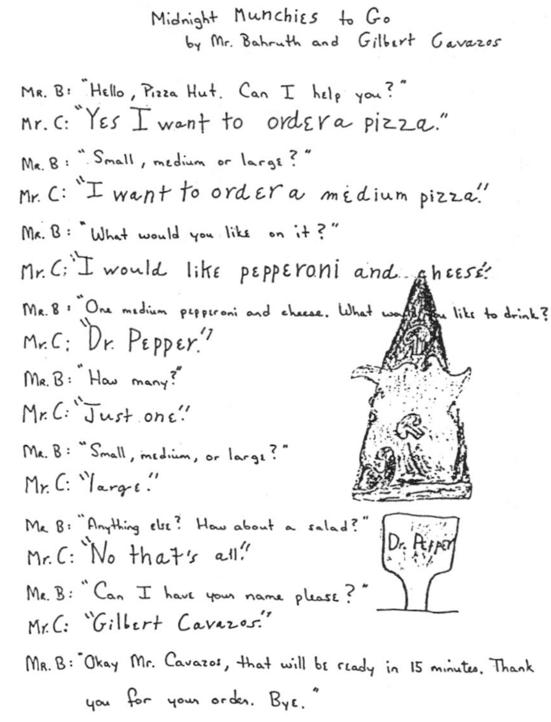

Midnight Munchies to Go
by Mr. Bahruth and Gilbert Cavazos

Mr. B: "Hello, Pizza Hut. Can I help you?"

Mr. C: "Yes I want to order a pizza."

Mr. B: "Small, medium or large?"

Mr. C: "I want to order a medium pizza."

Mr. B: "What would you like on it?"

Mr. C: "I would like pepperoni and cheese."

Mr. B: "One medium pepperoni and cheese. What would you like to drink?"

Mr. C: "Dr. Pepper."

Mr. B: "How many?"

Mr. C: "Just one."

Mr. B: "Small, medium, or large?"

Mr. C: "large."

Mr. B: "Anything else? How about a salad?"

Mr. C: "No that's all."

Mr. B: "Can I have your name please?"

Mr. C: "Gilbert Cavazos."

Mr. B: "Okay Mr. Cavazos, that will be ready in 15 minutes. Thank you for your order. Bye."

---

**figure 4–3b**

City-hall
by: Christina Benavidez and Maria anna Rodriguez

Maria: "Hello."

Christina: "City hall Mrs. Benavidez speaking who is this"?

Maria: "Mrs. treviño"?

Christina: "May I help you"

Maria: "Yes"

Christina: "What can I do for you"

Maria: "may I pay some Bills on monday"?

Christina: "How much do you want to give down"?

Maria: "I am going to give $20.00 on monday."

Christina: "OK Thats fine."

Maria: "on friday I am going to give you $31.00."

Christina: "OK Can you come over her I need to talk to you"?

Maria: "yes I can."

Christina: "Can you come on Thursday?"

Maria: "Okay by."

Christina: "have a nice day."

---

a bill payer, Alex and Francisco assumed the roles of doctor and patient, and Patricia and Alejandra created a conversation between a policewoman and a robbery victim. (The transcribed conversations of these three teams are shown in Figures 4–3b through 4–3d.) Additional conversations occurred between the school nurse and a mother,

**figure 4–3c**

The Doctor

by Alex Rodriquez + Francisco Garza

Alex: "Hello this is Dr. Rodriquez."

Francisco: "Hy Doc. I was painting the house and the dog push the latter and I fall down and I brok my leg."

Alex: "When was this"

Francisco: "It was this morning."

Alex: "how bad is the Leg."

Francisco: "I don't know can you come to my hoose."

Alex: "I don't know."

Francisco: "Come and pick me up."

Alex: "what time."

Francisco: "What time do you get out?"

Alex: "at 6:30 that will be ok."

Francisco: "Good bye."

Alex: "bye."

**figure 4–3d**

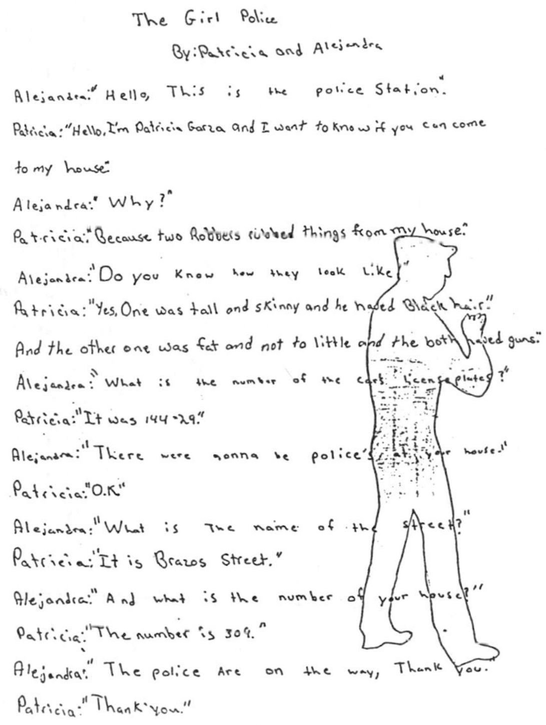

The Girl Police

By: Patricia and Alejandra

Alejandra: "Hello, This is the police Station."

Patricia: "Hello, I'm Patricia Garza and I want to know if you can come to my house."

Alejandra: "Why?"

Patricia: "Because two Robbers robbed things from my house."

Alejandra: "Do you Know how they look Like."

Patricia: "Yes. One was tall and skinny and he had Black hair."

And the other one was fat and not to little and the both had guns."

Alejandra: "What is the number of the cars license plates?"

Patricia: "It was 144-29."

Alejandra: "There were gonna be police at your house."

Patricia: "O.K."

Alejandra: "What is The name of the street?"

Patricia: "It is Brazos Street."

Alejandra: "And what is the number of your house?"

Patricia: "The number is 308."

Alejandra: "The police Are on the way, Thank You.

Patricia: "Thank you."

a pet owner and a veterinarian, and a homeowner and a plumber. These collaboratively written papers were published in a book, with a cover and a table of contents, entitled *Conversation Pieces*. The conversations were not assigned but chosen and generated by students.

### What does it mean, "He kicked the bucket?"

Idioms are a source of play. Language users like to construct and make up idioms. These children were no different, but idioms have often presented a problem for language learners, and they did for these limited-English-proficient students. They had difficulty determining the meaning of idioms, when heard or when encountered in their reading. One student inquired, "What does it mean, 'kick the bucket'?"

The class therefore investigated the nature of idioms, portraying their literal interpretations through drawings and then annotating these drawings with their idiomatic interpretations. They went to adults in the community to gather idioms. The principal gave them "clean your plow" and "fix your wagon." Some of the children contributed more than one selection to a book they entitled, *The What Did You Say? Handbook of Idioms.* Several of these contributions are shown in Figures 4–4a through 4–4f.

A class may have its own private language, its own idioms. The last idiom shown (Figure 4–4f), a class idiom, was explained by Roman. Even though asked not to, children sometimes forgot and wandered around the classroom, especially during those times when small-group activity was taking place. Robert's query "Are you on tour?" could only mean one thing to Roman and the others.

By explaining idioms with drawings, the children became aware of figurative as well as literal meanings and the differences between them. In Spanish, the children could decipher many of the *modismos*, or idioms, but in English, their second language, they had problems.

The decoding of idioms, and the children's fascination with them, continued. Several new idioms were discussed weekly and drawings of their literal as well as their figurative meanings were posted on the

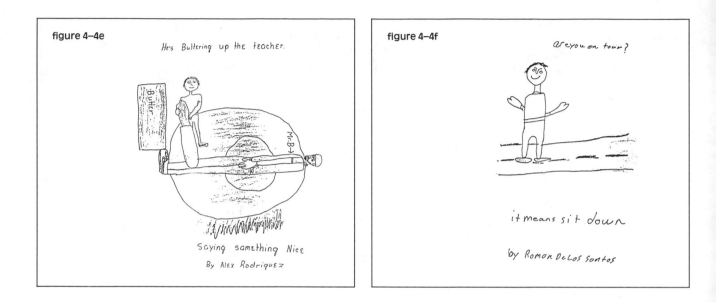

figure 4–4e

He's Buttering up the teacher.

Butter

Mr. B→

Saying samething Nice

By Alex Rodriquez

figure 4–4f

are you on tour?

it means sit down

by Roman DeLos Santos

bulletin board. They began to employ idioms in their writing. They incorporated them into their speaking and found them in their readings. Attention to idiomatic language contributed to increased comprehension when they read. They had fun spotting idioms in use outside the classroom. One, "Don't Mess with Texas," meaning "Don't Discard Litter," was itself a source of class discussion about ecology and food chains. The children were becoming observers of idioms in action: why they were used and how they came about.

## I dare you . . .

An assignment to publish a book on crazy and absurd recipes stirred creative powers for another form of play with writing. Maria's

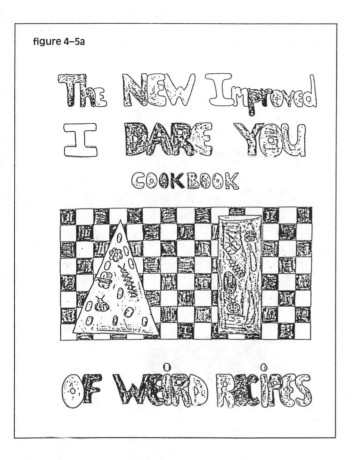

figure 4–5a

"Chocolate Pizza," Amy's "Hotdog Split," Francisco's "Ice Cream Cheese," Christina's "Cockroach with Beans, Ice Cream, and Bread," and Alex's "Taco with Ice Cream," among other zany dishes, led to *The I Dare You Cookbook of Weird Recipes*. The children, pleased with their book, asked to write another. Four months later, a sequel appeared (see the cover, shown in Figure 4–5a).

figure 4–5b

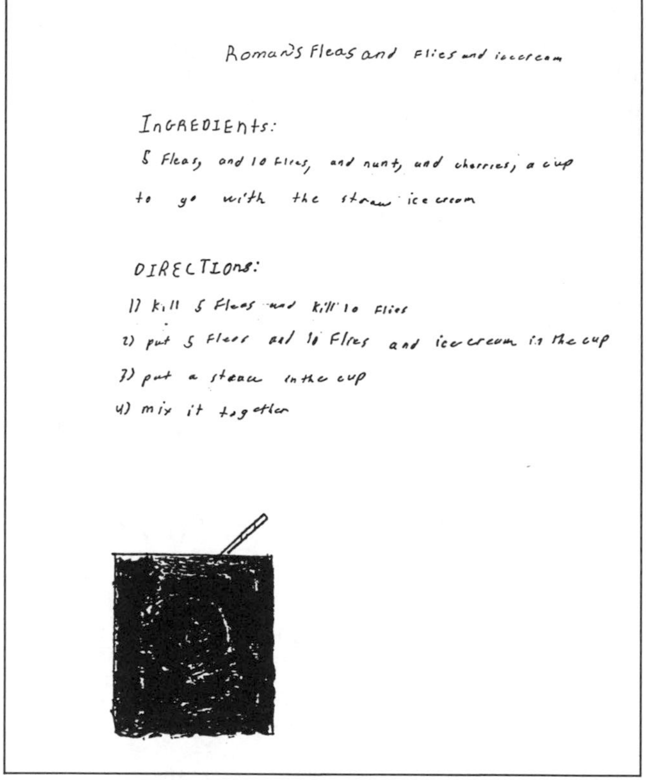

Roman's Fleas and Flies and iccoream

INGREDIENTS:
5 Fleas, and 10 Flies, and nuts, and cherries, a cup
to go with the straw ice cream

DIRECTIONS:
1) kill 5 Fleas and kill 10 Flies
2) put 5 Fleas and 10 Flies and ice cream in the cup
3) put a straw in the cup
4) mix it together

figure 4–5c

David's Snake taco

INGREDIENTS:
One body of a snake, a box of tobacco, maggot.

DIRECIIONS:
1. Get a body of a snake.
2. Gut the body in the middle.
3. Put the tobacco in top of the body of the snake
4. Put the maggots on top of the. tobacco.

Francisco perched a butterfly on his strawberry in his coconut recipe. Roman contributed an entry combining fleas and flies with ice cream (Figure 4–5b), David thought a snake taco would be delicious (Figure 4–5c), and Christina added a cockroach to hers (Figure 4–5d). Rene made a milkshake with "one big fat scorpion"; Gilbert

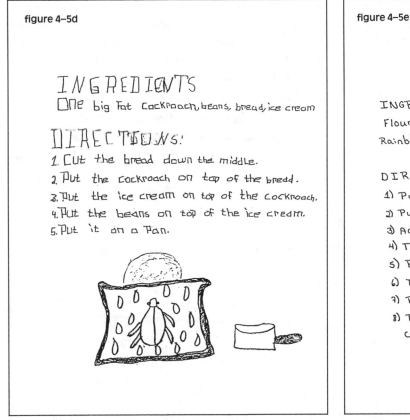

figure 4–5d

INGREDIENTS
One big Fat Cockroach, beans, bread, ice cream

DIRECTIONS:
1. Cut the bread down the middle.
2. Put the cockroach on top of the bread.
3. Put the ice cream on top of the cockroach.
4. Put the beans on top of the ice cream.
5. Put it on a Pan.

figure 4–5e

Norma's cakes

INGREDIENTS:
Flour, Ice cream, cherries, leaves, grass, ants, Rainbow, Beard.

DIRECTIONS:
1) Put flour in a pot.
2) Put leaves on top of the flour.
3) Add grass with ants.
4) Then put in a Rainbow.
5) Put in the Beard of MR. Bahruth.
6) Then put in the oven.
7) Put the Ice cream on top.
8) Then put the cherries on top of the Ice cream.

added eyeballs taken from horses to an ostrich egg omelette; and Norma made a cake featuring Robert's beard (Figure 4–5e).

This class activity added another dimension to becoming fluent readers and writers: organization. The ingredients in the recipes were listed first, followed by process statements in sequence, with eating occurring last. Organization schemata specific to various content areas are important in writing and reading. This assignment facilitated the ability to write about events that happen in sequence, a form of writing found in content areas. Handwriting also improved. It not only became more legible but even more assertive.

The impetus to publish as well as the motivation to read and critically comment on the writing of their classmates, continued. The books, including the designs on the cover, became more substantial. The children suggested titles for additional volumes, including one on aliens.

### Everything you always wanted to know about . . .

Writing with sufficient descriptive detail was difficult at first. The lack of elaboration is a mark of a developing, perhaps inexperienced writer. In writing conferences, the children were always asked to add details, to clarify, to elaborate; they learned that readers expect details from writers. Convinced that details were important, the children willingly began to draft papers on the theme "Everything You Wanted to Know About Aliens but Were Afraid to Ask."

The papers that went into this book, the cover of which is shown in Figure 4–6a, involved two children collaborating, one as writer, the other as illustrator. The writer had to include enough information so that the illustrator could draw an accurate and detailed figure. In critiquing written drafts, the illustrator could ask the writer to include additional information; the writer could critique the picture to see whether the artist had included all details. Each entry was a reading lesson; the artist had to be accurate or incur the displeasure of the author.

figure 4–6a

figure 4–6b

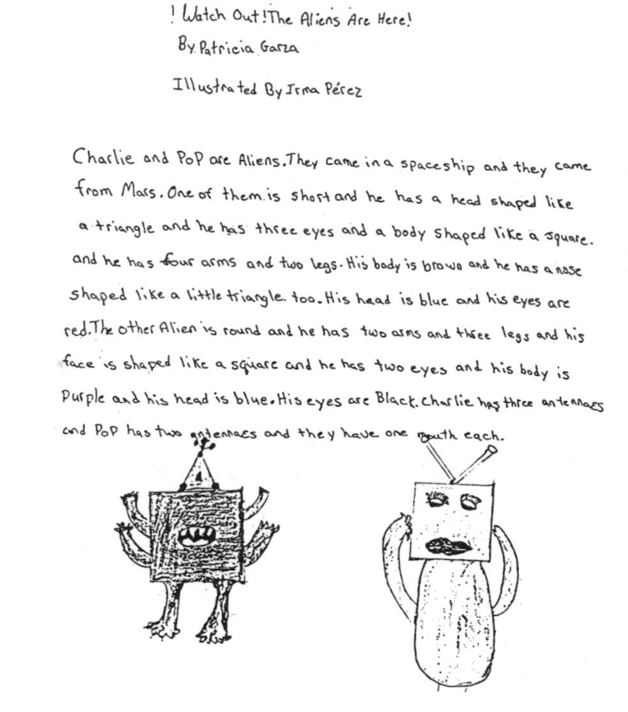

! Watch Out! The Aliens Are Here!
By Patricia Garza

Illustrated By Irma Pérez

Charlie and Pop are Aliens. They came in a spaceship and they came from Mars. One of them is short and he has a head shaped like a triangle and he has three eyes and a body shaped like a square. and he has four arms and two legs. His body is brown and he has a nose shaped like a little triangle. too. His head is blue and his eyes are red. The other Alien is round and he has two arms and three legs and his face is shaped like a square and he has two eyes and his body is Purple and his head is blue. His eyes are Black. charlie has three antennaes and Pop has two antennaes and they have one mouth each.

figure 4–6c

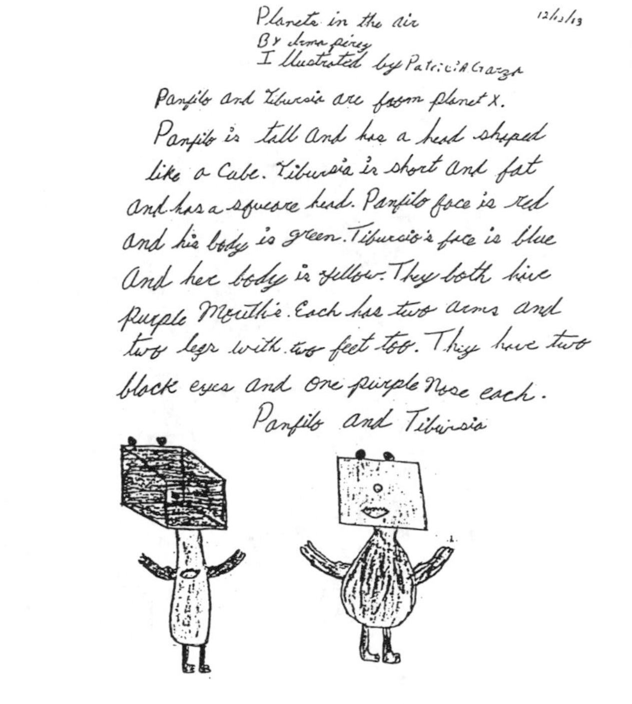

Planeta in the air                    12/3/13
By Irma pérez
I llustrated by Patricia Garza

Panfilo and Tiburcia are from planet X. Panfilo is tall and has a head shaped like a Cube. Tiburcia is short and fat and has a square head. Panfilo face is red and his body is green. Tiburcia's face is blue and her body is yellow. They both have purple Mouthis. Each has two arms and two legs with two feet too. They have two black eyes and one purple Nose each.
           Panfilo and Tiburcia

Some of the results of these collaborations are shown in Figures 4–6b through 4–6g. Notice that Francisco (Figure 4–6d) includes a description that serves to keep the two aliens apart, even indicating that "Po has seven hairs up." Alex (Figure 4–6e) and Christina

figure 4–6d

Po and Pe
by Francisco Garza
Illustration by Apolinar Garcia

Po and Pe are aliens. Po has four purple
arms and hands. He has six orange legs. He has
two yellow eyes. He has one red mouth. He has a
brown head shaped like a circle. Pe has two
yellow eyes. He has one green mouth. He has
four orange arms and hands. Pe and Po both have
pink bodies shaped like a square. Pe has a brown
head like a cube. He has six skinny blue legs. Pe
and Po both have one black tail like a snake.
Po has seven hairs up. Po and Pe both have black
nose like a pencil.

figure 4–6e

The Aliens
by Alex Rodriguez
Illustrated by David Valdez

Zo + EEk are from planet B. Zo
has a yellow square head.
EEk has a green trapezoid
head. Zo has a blue circle
body. EEk has a red cyLinder
body. Zo has four eyes. EEk
has four eyes too. Zo has
two green legs. EEk has three
purple Legs and Zo has three
pink arms. EEk has two
orange arms. and Zo has
a mouth. EEk has a mouth too
a red mouth.

(Figure 4–6f) each include a number of concepts they had learned in
a geometry unit, and both they and their illustrators have to be
accurate. Gilbert (Figure 4–6g) writes of aliens who have "no
stomach," but that's not a problem for Rene!

figure 4–6f

Aliens from the Moon
by Christina Benavidez
Illustrated by Alejandra Pérez

T and TO came from the moon. T has one blue eye and TO has two red eyes and T has a yellow mouth and TO has a red mouth. T has an orange nose shaped like a cylinder. TO has a pink nose shaped like a square. TO has four purple arms shaped like crows. TO has six green arms shaped triangles. T has a green head shaped like a circle. T has a blue body shaped like a ball. TO has a red body shaped like a cylinder. T has four orange legs. TO has two yellow legs.

figure 4–6g

Mr. Muscles + Mr. Crab
by Gilbert Cavazos
Illustrated by Rene Ramon

Mr. Muscles + Mr. Crab are from Planet M. They are the same size. Mr. Muscles is bigger because he has large antennas. They both have heads, they have no stomach and they have no hair. Mr. Crab has eleven arms and Mr. Muscles has two arms. They have two legs but Mr. Muscles has two crab legs + Mr. Crab has two horse legs.

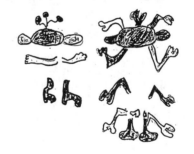

## Our outing

Accuracy and elaboration were skills with which the children now identified. They knew what it meant to address a reading audience. They could identify detail and explain the reason for detail in the books they were reading. They could in turn advise their classmates on how much detail to include in their papers. It was easy then, and fun, especially after writing about aliens, to write about their experiences on a field trip to a planetarium and to include as much detail as they thought necessary to lend credence to their papers and experience.

The field trip to the planetarium at San Antonio Community College included a presentation on the origin, shape, and growth of the universe. A narrative of each child's experiences appeared in a book entitled *Our Outing*. Many combined their experiences at the planetarium with recreation and lunch at the local park. The titles of individual pieces indicate different interests and focuses:

When We Stop in the Rest Area
The Planetarium
The Park
In the Bus
At the House
Our Field Trip
We Went to San Antonio

Apolinar wrote a short summary about the events at the planetarium (Figure 4–7a), while Jaime and Lisa wrote about the park where they had lunch and played afterwards (Figures 4–7b and 4–7c). Larry also wrote about the park, but did devote several lines to a description of the planetarium (Figure 4–7d). Amy, Norma, and Christina wrote about both (Figures 4–7e, 4–7f, and 4–7g).

While writing about the trip was fun, it required the ability to summarize, a writing skill useful in content-area writing assignments.

figure 4–7a

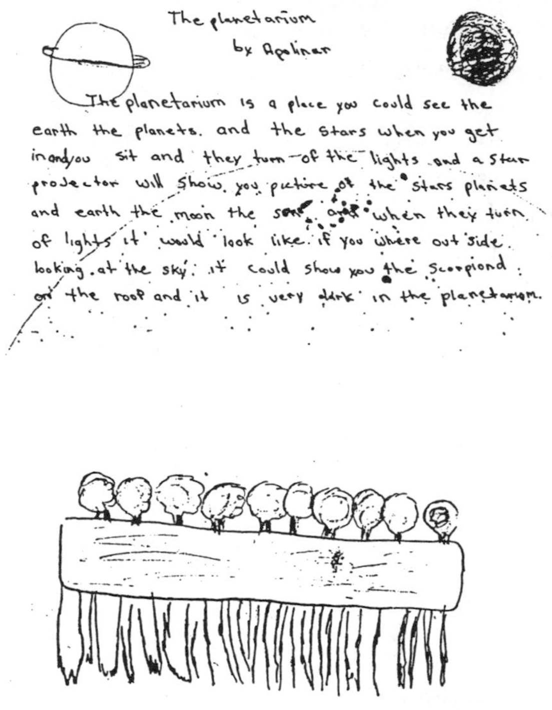

The planetarium
by Apolinar

The planetarium is a place you could see the earth the planets. and the stars when you get in and you sit and they turn of the lights and a star projector will show you picture of the stars planets and earth the moon the sun and when they turn of lights it would look like if you where out side looking at the sky. it could show you the scorpiond on the roof and it is very dark in the planetarium.

figure 4–7b

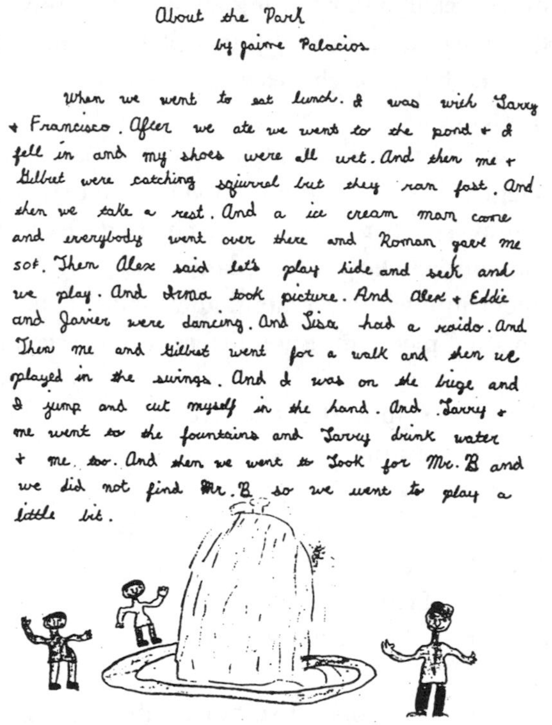

About the Park
by Jaime Palacios

When we went to eat lunch. I was with Larry + Francisco. After we ate we went to the pond + I fell in and my shoes were all wet. And then me + Gilbert were catching squirrel but they ran fast. And then we take a rest. And a ice cream man come and everybody went over there and Roman gave me sot. Then Alex said let's play hide and seek and we play. And Irma took picture. And Alex + Eddie and Javier were dancing. And Lisa had a raido. And Then me and Gilbert went for a walk and then we played in the swings. And I was on the huge and I jump and cut myself in the hand. And Larry + me went to the fountains and Larry drink water + me too. And then we went to look for Mr. B and we did not find Mr. B so we went to play a little bit.

The students were writing here partially about what they had learned. Such writing led into the "public" writing required by the school, the transactional, academically directed writing that children must learn if they are to succeed in school.

**figure 4–7c**

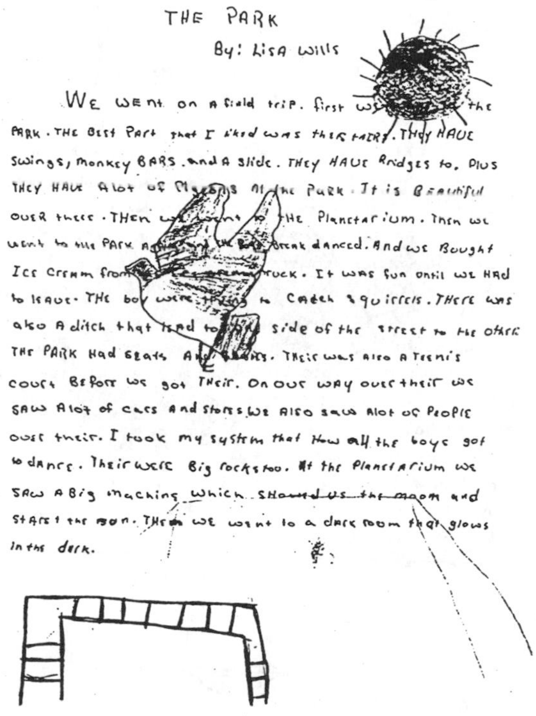

THE PARK
By: Lisa Wills

WE WENT on a field trip. first w... the PARK. THE BEST PART that I liked was their PARK. THEY HAVE swings, monkey BARS, and A slide. THEY HAVE bridges to. plus THEY HAVE A lot of Places At the PARK. It is Beautiful OVER there. THEN w... to THE PlanetARium. Then we went to the PARK ag... break danced. And we Bought Ice Cream fro... truck. It was fun until we HAD to leave. THE boy w... Catch squirrels. THERE was also A ditch that... side of the street to the other. THE PARK HAD seats A... ... THEre was also A Teeni's court Before we got their. On our way over their we saw A lot of cars and stores. We AlSo saw Alot of PEOPle over their. I took my system that How all the boys got to dance. Their were Big rocks too. At the PlanetARium we saw A Big maching which shOwed us the moon and starst the sun. Then we went to a dark room that glows in the dark.

**figure 4–7d**

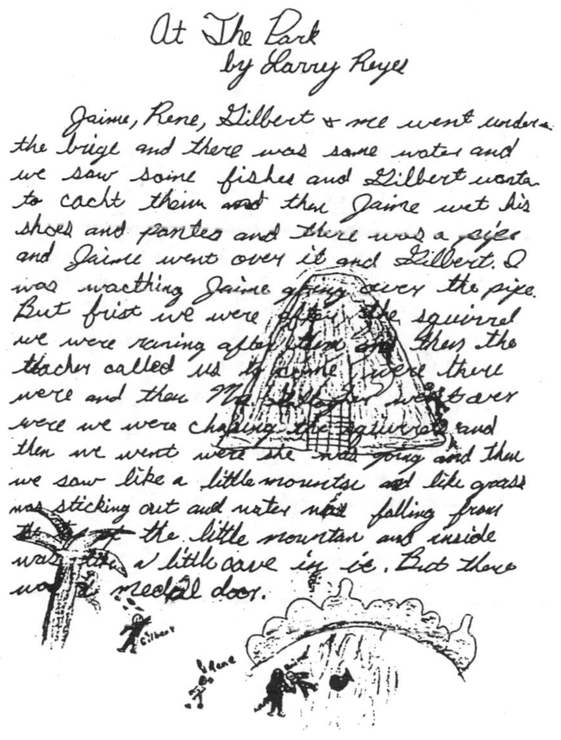

At The Park
by Harry Reyes

Jaime, Rene, Gilbert & me went under the bridge and there was some water and we saw some fishes and Gilbert wanted to cacht them and then Jaime wet his shoes and pantes and there was a pipe and Jaime went over it and Gilbert. I was wacthing Jaime going over the pipe. But frist we were after the squirrel we were runing after them and then the teacher called us ... there were and then Mr. ... ... were we were chasing the squirrel and then we went were she was going and then we saw like a little mountse and like grass was sticking out and water was falling from the little mountan and inside was ... a little cave in it. But there was a rectal door.

# I am a dreamer

Writing for fun continued. One day toward the end of May, just before dismissal for the summer, Jaime inquired in his journal, "Can we write a book about dreams?" When it was suggested in class

figure 4–7e

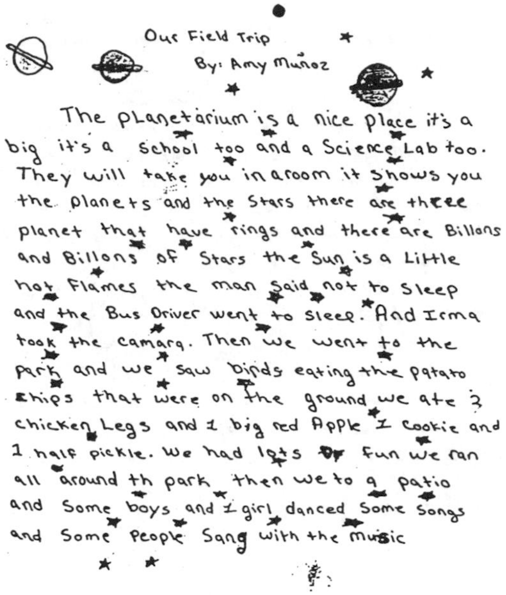

Our Field Trip
By: Amy Muñoz

The pLanetarium is a nice place it's a big it's a school too and a Science Lab too. They will take you in a room it shows you the planets and the stars there are three planet that have rings and there are Billons and Billons of Stars the Sun is a Little hot Flames the man said not to sleep and the Bus Driver went to sleep. And Irma took the camarq. Then we went to the park and we saw birds eating the patato chips that were on the ground we ate 3 chicken Legs and 1 big red Apple I cookie and 1 half pickle. We had lots of fun we ran all around th park then we to a patio and some boys and 1 girl danced Some Songs and Some people Sang with the music

figure 4–7f

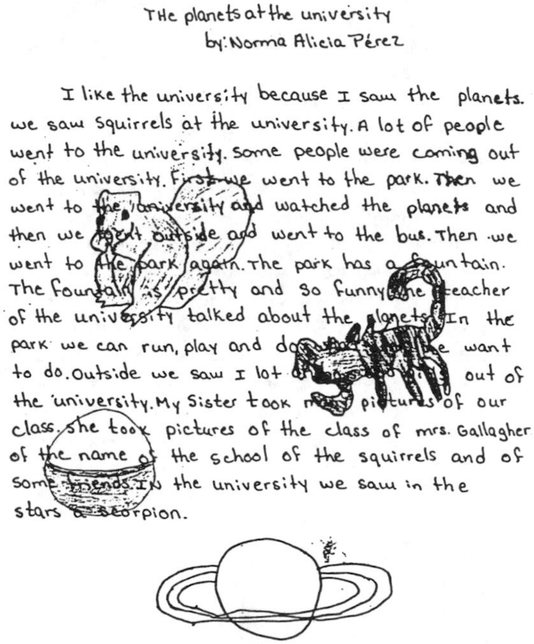

THe planets at the university
by: Norma Alicia Pérez

I like the university because I saw the planets. we saw squirrels at the university. A lot of people went to the university. some people were coming out of the university. First we went to the park. Then we went to the university and watched the planets and then we went outside and went to the bus. Then we went to the park again. the park has a fountain. The fountain is pretty and so funny the teacher of the university talked about the planets. In the park we can run, play and do what we want to do. Outside we saw I lot of cars out of the university. My Sister took many pictures of our class. she took pictures of the class of mrs. Gallagher of the name of the school of the squirrels and of some friends. In the university we saw in the stars a scorpion.

discussion, the children agreed. All were interested in dreams; all had dreams; and all had something to say about a particular dream they once had. Some children entitled their descriptions simply "My Dream." Others were more detailed and descriptive:

figure 4–7g

Our trip at the Planetarium
by: Christina Benavidez

My favorite Part was at the Park because we ate at the Park and then we went to the swings and at the slides. And then we went on the bus to go to the Planetarium. We saw the sky on top of the roof and the stars and then we saw the sun and the moon we saw everything it was fun. And then Irma took Pictures of Norma and then she took pictures of Norma. Then the ice cream man came and then we bought some ice cream. We saw some squirrels up on top of the tree we were trying to get the Squirrels it was hard to get them.

A Scary Dream

My Dream about a Volcano

In Heaven

My Funny Dream

My Favorite Dream

Nightmare

My Spider Man Dream

My Lion Dream

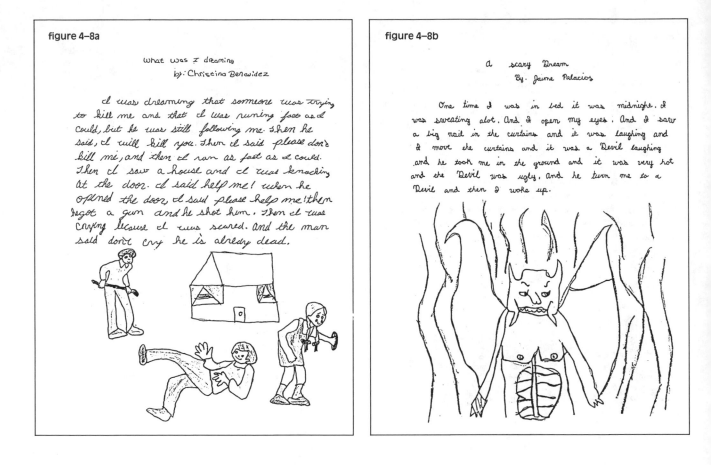

figure 4–8a

What was I dreaming
by: Christina Benavidez

I was dreaming that someone was trying to kill me and that I was runing fast as I could, but he was still following me. Then he said, I will kill you. Then I said please don't kill me, and then I ran as fast as I could. Then I saw a house and I was knocking at the door. I said help me! when he opened the door, I said please help me! then I got a gun and he shot him. Then I was crying because I was scared. And the man said don't cry he is already dead.

figure 4–8b

a scary Dream
By: Jaime Palacios

One time I was in bed it was midnight. I was sweating alot. And I open my eyes. And I saw a big nail in the curtains and it was laughing and I move the curtains and it was a Devil laughing and he took me in the ground and it was very hot and the Devil was ugly, and he turn me to a Devil and then I woke up.

Christina wrote about a dream that involved a chase (Figure 4–8a); Jaime also wrote about a scary dream (Figure 4–8b). Francisco wrote about a volcano (Figure 4–8c). Norma wrote of dreams coming true (Figure 4–8d). In telling about their dreams, several students wrote

figure 4–8c

My Dream About A Volcano
by Francisco Garza

I was seeing a scarry movie and then I went to sleep. I dreamed that we were close to a volcano. Two weeks later the volcano started to trow rocks and hot lava. All the houses were falling down. The dirt was opening to the side and people were falling down. Some people were safe because they went far away out of the town. All the people that were safe they made a little town. Everybody was happy. Then my mom came and woke me up. Then I forgot everything. Then I washed my face and I brushed my teeth. Then I went to school happy and safe.

figure 4–8d

My dreams that it was true.
by Norma Alicia Pérez

Once upon a time I was sleep and I was dreaming about my sister. And I got up and then my mother got up too. she told me what happed I said nothing. I was dreaming about Santos and my sister. I was dreaming that my sister she was in my house. she said no she is not here. O.K. I need to sleep you go to sleep too. And I was in my bed and then in a few minutes my sister came to my house. I said to my mother my dreams came true. And she said to my sister Norma dream that you came here and it came true.

stories with a beginning, a problem, and a resolution of the problem. Amy, for example, wrote a story, with a description of her dream and the resolution of the problems posed in that dream, accompanied by dialogue (see Figure 4–8e).

figure 4–8e

My Silly Dream
By: Amy Munoz

I had just gone to bed, and as I was falling asleep. I guess I must have really gone to sleep, cause I dreamed that I was lying in my bed. And that I got up to answer the door. As I opened the door I didn't see anybody. But I swear I had heard somebody knock. So I shut the door and I went back to try to sleep. But then again I heard a loud knock on my window. And this time I asked first said who is it? and the thing or who ever was knocking on the window kept saying it's me. I said who. It answer you know. So I got up. It looked like Mr. Bahruth but he looked like a frog man. He said, open the window Amy! So I just stood there not knowing what to do. So he tried to open the window himself. I was felling so scared I jumped out of bed, and closed the window on him very fast that I chopped off his green fingers. His fingers started to move toward me, so I jumped to bed and covered my face. Then all off a sudden I felt somebody touching me. I screamed out loud, and I

figure 4–8e (continued)

My Silly Dream
By: Amy Munoz

uncovered my face and I yelled Leave me alone! I was all suprise to find, it was my mom waking me up to get ready for school. So I said mom I really did fall asleep after all. But Boy did I have a night mare. I was an ugly one. I'm glad it was you waking me up mom not those green fingers and mom said, What green fingers? Never mind mom, It was only a dream. So I went very very happy. Knowing that it was only a silly dream. In the morning I told my friend how Mr. Bahruth looked like. This was how he looked Like. He had a big head like a frog. with three big eyes no nose but a mouth from ear to ear and 2 ears like Dumbo the Elephant

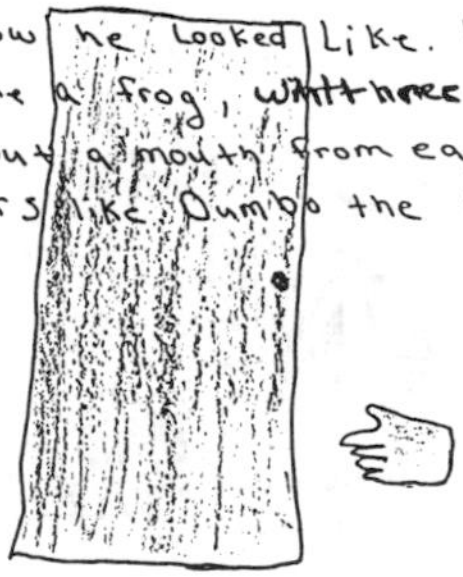

## Bestiaries

From dreams to animals was an easy step to take. Children at this age are fascinated by animals. Many of the students owned pets; many had been to the circus; and most had the opportunity to view cartoons and feature films with animals as the main characters. Robert brought into the classroom a number of books on animals from the library and his personal collection, and the children set about reading them. They decided to publish their own books on animals. They first published an accurate bestiary (discussed in Chapter 5) and followed that with a book they entitled *Make-Believe Bestiaries*, a description of animals they had created in their imaginations.

Verbal play appeared in these descriptions. For example, Christina wrote about *Armadilbirs* (a cross between armadillos, animals resident to the Southwest, and birds) (Figure 4–9a). Larry wrote of the *Liuck*, an animal that could kill any animal, "like the Tigebear" (Figure 4–9b). Francisco, Larry's best friend, described his *Tigebear* as killing any animal, including the Liuck (Figure 4–9c). Apolinar's *Cheetahcat* could kill "the liucks and the tigerbears to" (Figure 4–9d). Since his selection appeared as the last essay in the last book, *Odds and Ends*, Apolinar had the last word in this verbal battle!

A child writes papers to be read. There is a difference between writing to a limited audience—a teacher who will evaluate, judge, and return the paper with a grade, along with comments of what went wrong—and writing for a wider audience that includes peers. The children soon found that writing, like reading, was intellectually invigorating. Writing enlivened the school day. At the same time it was collaborative. Instead of asking only the teacher about problems they encountered in their writing, writers turned to their classmates for help, advice, and solutions. Robert asked the children to read their papers to at least three of their classmates and solicit suggestions. He had specific times for gathering the children together into *helping circles* to read their writing, to react to what they heard from others, and to offer solutions or advice. Mr. B. gave the students

figure 4–9a

Armadilbirs

by: Christina Benavidez

Madilbirs are weird animals. And they could eat meat, grass, and leaf. Armadillbirs do not run fast but they could hide in a hole. His tail is not long. And you could kill the Armadilbir and you could eat them. And you could get them from the tail when you kill them but they can escape. And when they see a snake they run from them. The shaped of the armadilbir body is a bird and the shaped of the head is a armadilbirs.

figure 4–9b

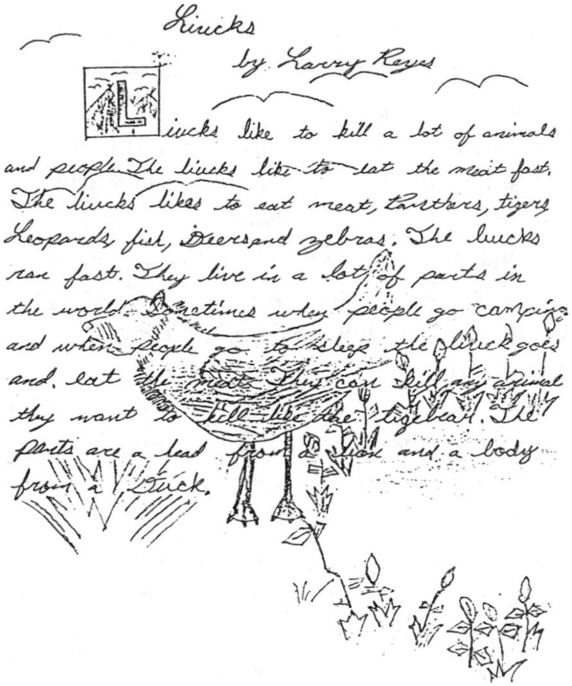

Liucks

by Larry Reyes

Liucks like to kill a lot of animals and people. The liucks like to eat the meat fast. The liucks likes to eat meat, tirthers, tigers leopards, fish, deers and zebras. The liucks ran fast. They live in a lot of parts in the world. Sometimes when people go camping and when people go to sleep the liuck goes and eat the meat. They can kill any animal they want to kill the the tigebear. The parts are a head from a fox and a body from a Duck.

directions on how to help their classmates; some of the questions he urged them to ask or attend to were:

1. Is there a point to the writing?
2. Does the writer give details?
3. Is there a beginning and an end?

figure 4–9c

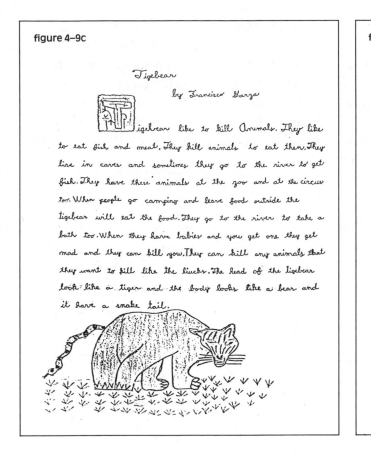

Tigebear

by Francisco Garza

Tigebear like to kill Animals. They like to eat fish and meat. They kill animals to eat them. They live in caves and sometimes they go to the river to get fish. They have these animals at the zoo and at the circus too. When people go camping and leave food outside the tigebear will eat the food. They go to the river to take a bath too. When they have babies and you get one they get mad and they can kill you. They can kill any animals that they want to kill like the liucks. The head of the tigebear look like a tiger and the body looks like a bear and it have a snake tail.

figure 4–9d

Cheetahcats

by Apolinar Garcia.

Cheetahcats are bobcats and a cheetah put together. the cheetahcats are 5feet high and 7 feet long they live in the moontains the eat small animals and it could kill the liuks and the the tigerbears to the cheetahcats are very strong they could jump a lake and run very fast. and the cheetahcats you could see them in winter sometimes you see them in spring. they could fight almost anithing. some times when people go camping and sleep at night the chetahcat goes and eat the food.

4. After hearing the writing, are you able to repeat or paraphrase it?
5. Did the writer ask for help?

Writing was both fun and difficult. It took sustained effort. Yet it was play: the children knew that they were using language to explore concepts and taking risks with language. At the same time they were increasing their literacy skills. Daiute (1989) reminds us that "as in other areas of human development, play is useful for writing development because children select their own themes and approaches" (663). This was exactly what the children were doing.

By writing for fun, under conditions that were playful and loving, the children were preparing to "write across the curriculum," to write about what they were learning in specific academic areas. It is to this writing that we now turn.

# chapter

*Gilbert discovers pieces*
*of the world*

*. . . it is impossible to teach content without knowing how*
*students think in the context of their daily lives,*
*without knowing what they know independently of school*
*so that we can, on the one hand, help them to know better*
*what they already know and, on the other,*
*teach them what they don't know yet. We cannot stop*
*taking into consideration the unfavorable material conditions*
*that many students of schools in marginalized areas*
*of the city experience: the precariousness*
*of their living quarters, the deficiency of their food,*
*the lack of reading activities in their daily lives*
*and of study in their schools,*
*the violence and death that they know almost intimately.*

Freire, *Ninth Letter*

Children who do not have the opportunity to write are denied a rich avenue to improved thinking and learning—the cognitive skills that can accrue from writing (Gere 1985, 5). Writing is an efficient tool for teaching the content areas. Robert's students read and discussed material from their social studies, science, and language arts texts. They extrapolated information from their texts, organized it, selected topics, wrote drafts, and read them to their classmates. They received feedback, revised, scheduled conferences with their teacher about their work, and prepared their final drafts for publication. As a result of this shared writing, the children also became teachers. Robert and his students individually could not possibly have known as much as they knew collectively.

*Thinking* and *learning* were the goals for the class, and as the students moved through the school year, they were provided challenging and meaningful opportunities to write, learn, and think:

1. Robert wished to promote fluency both in reading and writing. He met this goal by providing blocks of time during the school day when the class read from basals, library books, and texts. Each table of students constituted a reading group, and Robert listened to each student read orally at least twice a week. The students, along with Robert, also participated in sustained silent reading, reading for reports they were writing, and reading for pleasure.
2. Robert wanted reading and writing proficiency to improve at the same time learning and thinking were being fostered. He addressed these goals by discussing, in class and in the journals, what they were reading, writing, and learning and how they could improve even more.
3. Robert wanted to turn the students into enthusiastic, risk-taking

# five

writers, readers, and learners. He encouraged the students to take books home and read them to siblings and parents, to write, to share, and to publish. Reading and writing became a way of life, were not just isolated activities that occurred sporadically, without purpose.

Before he asked his students to write, Robert provided models for them and then wrote along with them. The dialogue journal (see Chapter 3) provided opportunities for risk-free writing, with few demands or restrictions and no overt corrections. Once the children were into the routine of journal writing, the first step had been taken. Cummins (1986) provides an additional reason for writing personally: "Ample opportunities for expressive writing appear to be particularly significant in promoting a sense of academic efficacy among minority students" (29).

The dialogue journal, and the writing activities that followed, accompanied by Robert's daily reading from a variety of sources, grew to daily and weekly times for expressing, communicating, and sharing, not only with Mr. B., but also with peers through *helping circles* (see Chapter 6) and class-published books. As they published and shared "fun" papers, the children began to write across the curriculum, on themes or topics selected from the state-mandated curriculum, including science, mathematics, geography, and history. This type of writing is often referred to as *academic writing*, and Britton (1982) calls it *transactional* to distinguish it from *expressive*, or personal, writing. Transactional writing, the "public language of schooling" (Genishi 1989, 511), is the writing demanded by the school: it informs, instructs, or persuades. Transactional language is language to "get something done" (Britton 1970, 169). When engaged in transactional writing, students write about topics beyond their personal experience. Atwell (1987) puts it thus:

*We use writing to discover what we know, think, and believe. We also use
writing as social discourse, to conduct transactions with the rest of the world,
sharing what we know, think, and believe. (106)*

Transactional and expressive writing (particularly with elementary-
age children) meld into one another. Personal and expressive musings
are mixed in with the transactional writing required in producing
essays and reports. Robert's students combined personal reflections
with information learned, as in their *Autobiographies of Not-Yet-Famous
Persons* (see Chapter 6). And in an earlier book, *Our Outing*, the
students combined what they had observed (transactional) with their
personal feelings about the events of that day (expressive).

Writing transactionally is difficult, and Robert of course did not say,
"All right, we have been writing expressively—we are now going to
write transactionally." He believed that it might be too difficult and
unproductive to have the children attempt to write transactional prose
on the adult model (Jacobs 1984, 362). Yet he wanted to demonstrate
that personal writing is different from academic writing, and while
the two can be combined, it is the ability to write transactionally that
leads to school success.

Once the students were writing, they were asked to write about
what they were learning. State-adopted textbooks provided demonstrations and examples of transactional writing strategies that authors
within the academic disciplines employ when writing about their
subjects. Robert described and illustrated for his class characteristics
of academic writing and demonstrated how writers use such strategies
as cause and effect, comparison and contrast, and problem and
solution to organize their work. These same strategies emerged in
the students' writing as they started to write about what they were
learning.

## Alphabet soup

The curriculum included a world geography unit. Robert helped each student select a country (again, the alphabet was the structural device, one country for every letter), become an "expert" on it, and write and share what he or she had learned. After determining the location of various countries and regions in the world and researching demographics, agriculture, industry, imports, and exports, they wrote about their findings and published their essays in *International Alphabet Soup*.

Gilbert selected the letter *V* and studied and wrote about Venezuela (see Figure 5–1a). Gilbert's organizational pattern is a collection of facts. He locates Venezuela and its principal city, and describes the monetary system, resources, language, and topography. He read about Venezuela; he wrote about it; and he showed in his work what he had learned. The information that Gilbert collected and organized into a paper was available to the entire class. The students learned from each other.

In his journal entry written when he was ill, Francisco requested the letter *C* because he wanted to write about "Cuetador." Robert responded that *C* had already been selected by a classmate, but that the letter *A* had been saved for him. Francisco wrote about Australia (see Figure 5–1b), using the concept of "continet" to describe Australia. His English, although not perfect, is meaningful: "They do coats with the sheeps." *They* also seems to be Francisco's possessive pronoun substituting for *their*, as in "They money is half dollors." Yet his imperfect English did not prevent him from writing and his classmates from reading his paper. Both Francisco and his classmates were involved in learning.

Not only did the students encounter information about countries of the world, they included drawings of the countries' flags. The first

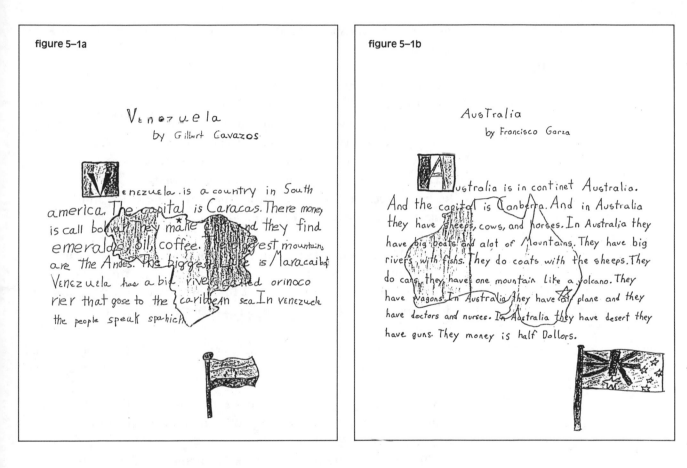

figure 5–1a

Venezuela
by Gilbert Cavazos

Venezuela is a country in South america. The capital is Caracas. There money is call bolivar. They make and they find emeralds, oil, coffee. The biggest mountains are the Andes. The biggest lake is Maracaibo. Venezuela has a big river called orinoco rier that gose to the caribbean sea. In venezuela the people speak spahich.

figure 5–1b

Australia
by Francisco Garza

Australia is in continet Australia. And the capital is Canberra. And in Australia they have sheeps, cows, and horses. In Australia they have big boats and alot of Mountains. They have big rivers with fishs. They do coats with the sheeps. They do cars, they have one mountain like a volcano. They have wagons. In Australia they have one plane and they have doctors and nurses. In Australia they have desert they have guns. They money is half Dollors.

word in their essays began with the *capítular* (see the description of the book entitled *Abecedario*, Chapter 4). They located their countries on the globe and included that information in their papers as well.

The following statements taken from their essays illustrate how geographical and spatial relationships, directions, and limitations were described:

| | |
|---|---|
| Maria Anna | Denmark is a country in northwest europe. |
| Alejandra | Ethiopia is a country in South West africa. |
| Norma | France is a country in Europe. |
| Amy | Hungary is a country in Central Europe. |
| Christina | Norway is a country in Northern Europe. |
| Lisa | Switzerland lies in the heart of Europe. |
| Monica | Iceland does not have a continent because it is an island. |
| Jessica | Turkey is a country in two continents. |

Kenya, described by Rosa (Figure 5–1c), is placed correctly near the Indian Ocean. She also gives an indication of its size. Some, as did Maria Anna (see Figure 5–1d), included a map with their descriptions. Maria Anna also described Denmark's proximity to Sweden.

The class could not find a country beginning with *X*, so they created one and gave it the name *Xanadu*. Figure 5–1e depicts that imaginary country.

When writing about their countries, the students identified the basic units of currency, though Rene wrote (about Zambia), "I didn't write the money because I didn't find it."

Their papers were first attempts at creating logical and cohesive meaning. Sentence-level errors were not totally eliminated. Misspellings (*fishs*, *sheeps*, *Febrery*, *Bubapest*, *blizzerd*) occurred, as well as grammatical errors ("United States is in continent North America"). These types of errors eventually decreased as competency in English increased. The students, through their collective research, read far

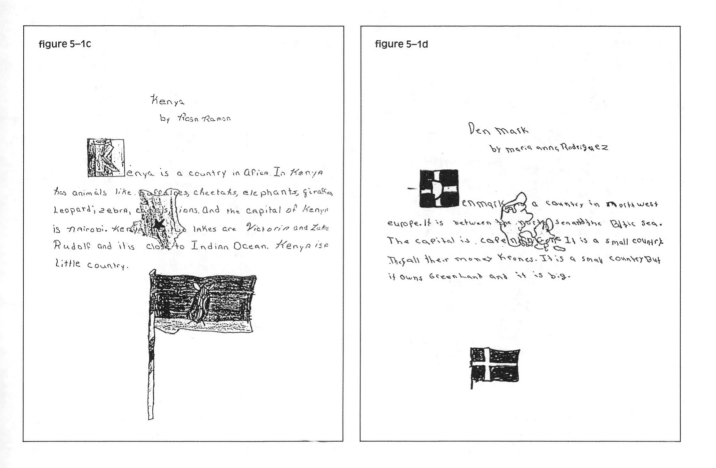

figure 5–1c

Kenya
by Rosa Ramon

Kenya is a country in Africa. In Kenya has animals like buffaloes, cheetahs, elephants, giraffes, Leopard, zebra, camels, lions. And the capital of Kenya is Nairobi. Kenya two lakes are Victoria and Lake Rudolf and it is close to Indian Ocean. Kenya is a Little country.

figure 5–1d

Den Mark
by maria anna Rodriguez

Denmark is a country in Northwest europe. It is between the North sea and the Baltic sea. The capital is Copenhagen. It is a small country. Theycall their money Krones. It is a small country But it owns GreenLand and it is big.

beyond what classroom texts alone offered. Appropriate library books were consulted, as were encyclopedias. The back inside cover of *International Alphabet Soup* lists a bibliography of the books that the students obtained for use as resources (see Figure 5–1f).

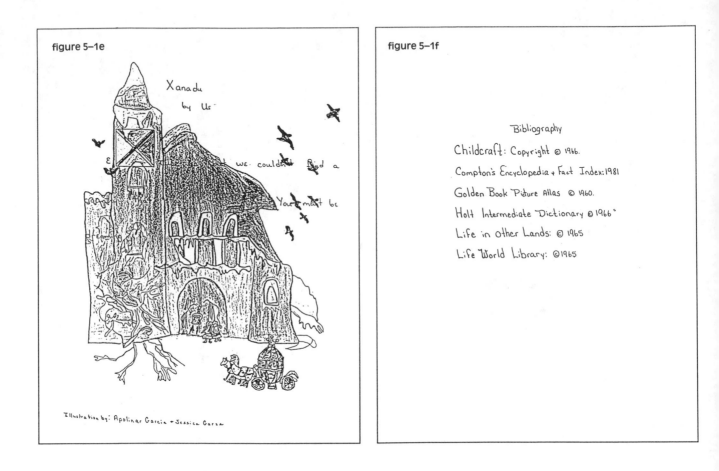

figure 5–1e

Xanadu
by Us

we couldn't find a
Your must be

Illustration by: Apolinar Garcia + Jessica Garza

figure 5–1f

Bibliography

Childcraft: Copyright © 1966.

Compton's Encyclopedia + Fact Index: 1981

Golden Book Picture Atlas © 1960.

Holt Intermediate Dictionary © 1966°

Life in other Lands: © 1965

Life World Library: ©1965

## Uncle Sam

While writing about world geography, the class began a related unit from the social studies curriculum and researched and wrote on the states making up the United States. After they chose their states, they drew maps, identified the state birds, flowers, and trees, and located the capitals. They learned about the topography (including major rivers) and ascertained the size of the population. Jessica wrote about Alaska and offered an explanation for the small population: "Less people there because its always snowing."

The fledgling researchers found the date of their state's admission to the Union and information on famous sons and daughters (we learn from Florencia that Douglas MacArthur was from Arkansas). They included the size of their state in relation to other states ("only three states are larger than Montana" and "Ohio is much larger than [the town where they lived]"). They spelled and pronounced unfamiliar place names: *Okefenokee Swamp, Tallahassee, King Kame-hameha, Boise, Picasso.*

They published the papers from this activity in a book (the cover is shown in Figure 5–2a). To demonstrate expository style, Robert wrote the introductory essay (Figure 5–2b). He explained the derivation of the appellation *Uncle Sam*, included a synopsis of the nation's early history, described the national symbols, and pointed out that "all of the states together make our country: The United States of America."

His essay is followed by similar descriptions of the states researched by the students. Gilbert wrote a description of New York State (Figure 5–2c) and, following Robert's example, included information on the flower, bird, and tree, as well as the origin of its nickname. Apolinar wrote about Vermont and included its connection to Robert's dog (Figure 5–2d).

Because they had selected countries and states by letter, the class not only reviewed alphabetical order, they also employed directional terms (*east, west, north,* and *south*) when describing the location of their state. They were not required to memorize the facts about each state,

**figure 5–2a**

United States
February 29, 1984

**figure 5–2b**

Introduction
by Mr. Bahruth

Uncle Sam is the nickname of the United States. The United States is a country in North America. There are two other countries on the North American continent; Canada to the north and Mexico to the south of "US."

Uncle Sam is over two hundred years old. Our first president was George Washington and the capital of the United States is named after him: Washington, D.C.

The national bird is the bald-headed eagle. It has dark brown feathers with white feathers on its head.

We live in Texas, which is only one of fifty states. The capital of Texas is Austin and each of the other states also has its own capital. All of the states together make our country: The United States of America.

but as they worked on their descriptions and talked with their classmates, they learned much.

## ABC bestiary

The letters-of-the-alphabet structural device was once again selected,

figure 5–2c

New York

by Gilbert Cavazos

New York is a state the state flower is the Rose. New York is in North America. The state bird is the blue bird. The state tree is the Sugar Maple tree. The capital of New York is Albany. One of the biggest bridges in New York is called Verrazano-Narrows bridge. The Niagara Falls is the famous water fall. Some of the highest skyscrapers are the Empire state building & the world Trabe center. The nickname of New York is The Empire State.

figure 5–2d

Vermont

by Apolinar Garcia

Vermont is a small state the capital is monpelier the state Flower is Red clover and the State tree is Sugarmaple. the State bird is Hermit trush. Vermont is one of the smallest states in the onion. the Nick Name is The Green Mountain State. And the name of the rivers are Winoski River and Missique. Mr. Bahruth bought his dog there his name is Bear in Spanish its oso he is a Bilingual dog he understands spanish & english.

this time for a science activity on animals. Some of the animals were inhabitants of the United States; others were not. Researching these animals necessitated using encyclopedias and other references found in the library. Robert encouraged the children to compile their research into reports incorporating their own observations. The students included facts describing their animal's physical

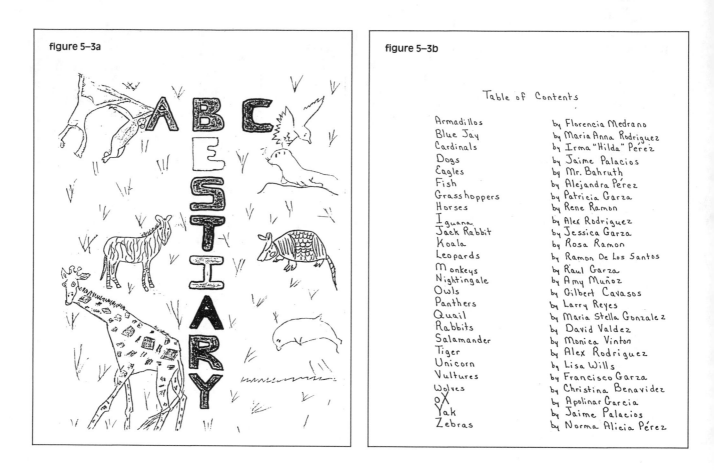

figure 5–3a

figure 5–3b

Table of Contents

| | |
|---|---|
| Armadillos | by Florencia Medrano |
| Blue Jay | by Maria Anna Rodriguez |
| Cardinals | by Irma "Hilda" Pérez |
| Dogs | by Jaime Palacios |
| Eagles | by Mr. Bahruth |
| Fish | by Alejandra Pérez |
| Grasshoppers | by Patricia Garza |
| Horses | by Rene Ramon |
| Iguana | by Alex Rodriguez |
| Jack Rabbit | by Jessica Garza |
| Koala | by Rosa Ramon |
| Leopards | by Ramon De Los Santos |
| Monkeys | by Raul Garza |
| Nightingale | by Amy Muñoz |
| Owls | by Gilbert Cavasos |
| Panthers | by Larry Reyes |
| Quail | by Maria Stella Gonzalez |
| Rabbits | by David Valdez |
| Salamander | by Monica Vinton |
| Tiger | by Alex Rodriguez |
| Unicorn | by Lisa Wills |
| Vultures | by Francisco Garza |
| Wolves | by Christina Benavidez |
| oX | by Apolinar Garcia |
| Yak | by Jaime Palacios |
| Zebras | by Norma Alicia Pérez |

characteristics, eating habits, habitat, as well as more unique information. The title of the book in which their papers are collected was *ABC Bestiary* (see Figure 5–3a). The book's table of contents (Figure 5–3b) lists the animals the children researched.

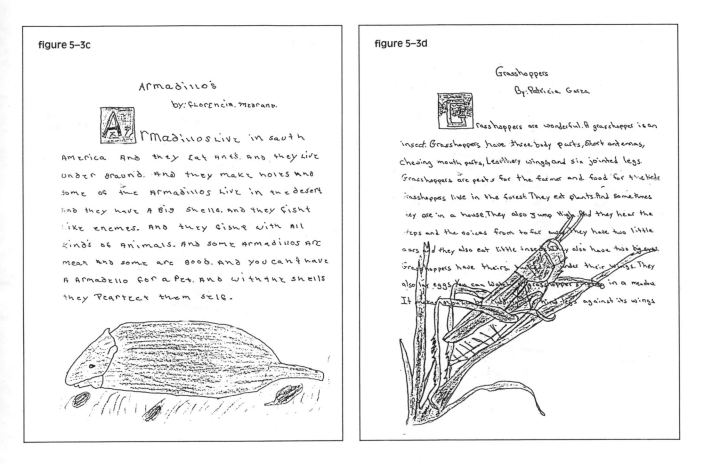

figure 5–3c

Armadillo's
by: Florencia. Medrano.

Armadillos live in south America and they eat ants. And they live under ground. And they make holes and some of the armadillos live in the desert and they have a big shells. and they fight like enemes. And they fight with all kinds of animals. And some armadillos are mean and some are good. And you can't have a armadillo for a pet. And with the shells they peartect them self.

figure 5–3d

Grasshoppers
By: Patricia Garza

Grasshoppers are wonderful. A grasshopper is an insect. Grasshoppers have three body parts, short antennas, chewing mouth parts, leathery wings, and six jointed legs. Grasshoppers are pests for the farmer and food for the birds. Grasshoppers live in the forest. They eat plants. And sometimes they are in a house. They also jump high. And they hear the steps and the voices from to far away. They have two little ears and they also eat little insects. They also have two big eyes. Grasshoppers have theirs ... under their wings. They also lay eggs. You can watch a grasshopper singing in a meadow. It makes a buzzing rubbing its hind legs against its wings

Florencia wrote about the armadillo (Figure 5–3c); Patricia called the grasshopper "wonderful" (Figure 5–3d); Maria Stella incorporated a metaphor to describe the quail's nose (Figure 5–3e); and Lisa used the unicorn to define the term *legend* (Figure 5–3f).

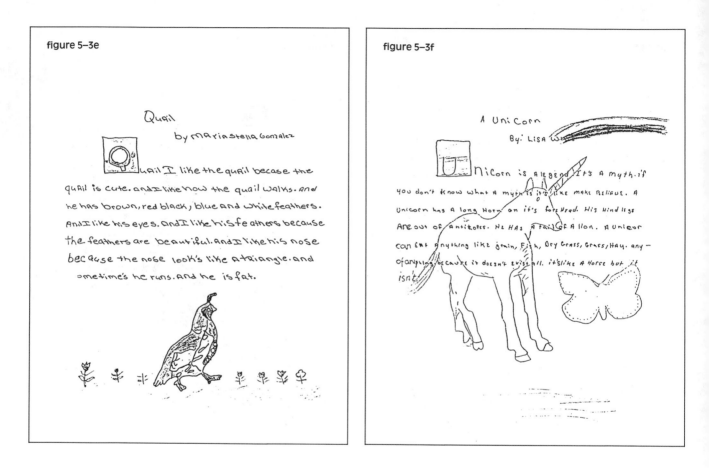

figure 5–3e

Quail

by Maria Stella Gonzalez

Quail I like the quail becase the quail is cute. and I like how the quail walks. And he has brown, red black, blue and white feathers. And I like his eyes. And I like his feathers because the feathers are beautiful. And I like his nose because the nose look's like a triangle. and sometime's he runs. And he is fat.

figure 5–3f

A Unicorn

By: Lisa W

Nicorn is a legend. It's a myth. if you don't know what a myth is it's like make Believe. A Unicorn has a long Horn on it's fore head. His Hind legs are out of antilopes. He has a tail of a llon. A Unicor can eat anything like grain, Fish, Dry Grass, Grass, Hay. any-of anything because it doesn't exist at all. it's like a Horse but it isn't.

Science writing continued. When the class was writing papers for *Small Wonders and Magic Machines*, they were grouped in pairs. Gilbert and Alex wrote about the tuning fork (Figure 5–4a), Maria Stella and Maria Anna about the human pulse. Some used the microscope to

figure 5–4a

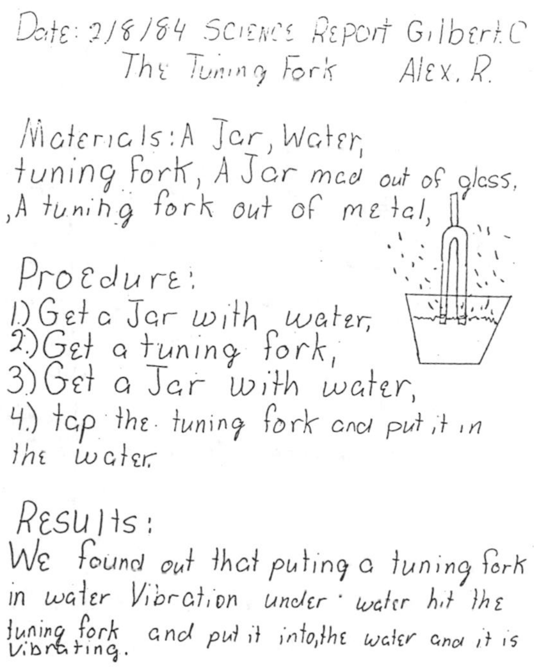

Date: 2/8/84 Science Report Gilbert C
The Tuning Fork    Alex. R.

Materials: A Jar, Water,
tuning fork, A Jar made out of glass,
, A tuning fork out of metal,

Proedure:
1.) Get a Jar with water,
2.) Get a tuning fork,
3.) Get a Jar with water,
4.) tap the tuning fork and put it in
the water.

Results:
We found out that putting a tuning fork
in water Vibration under water hit the
tuning fork and put it into the water and it is
vibrating.

figure 5–4b

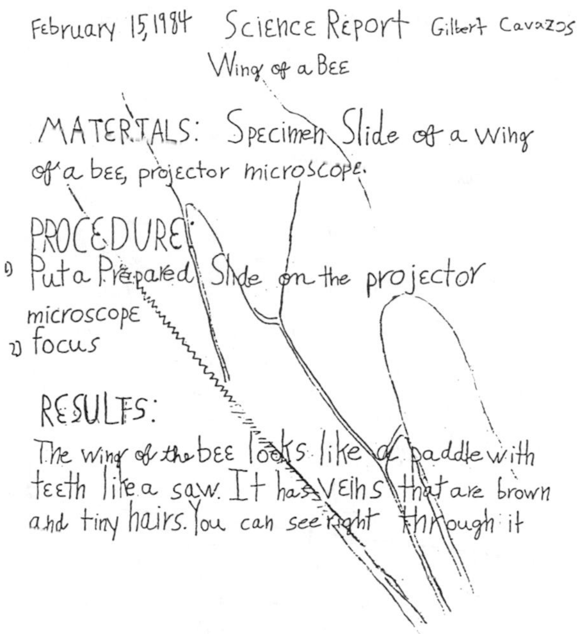

February 15, 1984    Science Report  Gilbert Cavazos
Wing of a Bee

MATERIALS: Specimen Slide of a wing
of a bee, projector microscope.

PROCEDURE:
1) Put a Prepared Slide on the projector
microscope
2) Focus

RESULTS:
The wing of the bee looks like a paddle with
teeth like a saw. It has veins that are brown
and tiny hairs. You can see right through it

describe the appearance of salt and sugar, the wing of a bee (Figure
5–4b), pheasant feathers, and snake scales. Jessica and Alex compared
hair from Robert's head with hair from his beard.

The science reports required the integration of language and

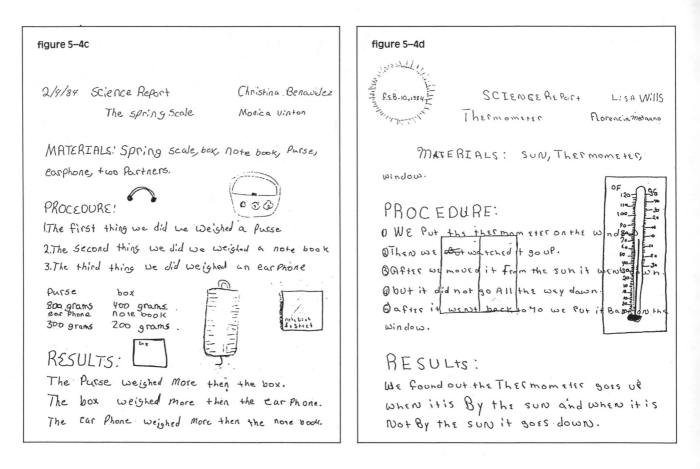

**figure 5–4c**

2/9/84   Science Report          Christina Benavidez
         The spring scale        Monica Vinton

MATERIALS: Spring scale, box, note book, Purse, earphone, two Partners.

PROCEDURE!
1. The first thing we did we weighed a Purse
2. The Second thing we did we weighed a note book
3. The third thing we did weighed an ear Phone

Purse        box
800 grams    400 grams
ear Phone    note book
300 grams    200 grams

RESULTS:
The Purse weighed More then the box.
The box weighed More then the ear Phone.
The ear Phone weighed More then the note book.

**figure 5–4d**

FEB. 10, 1984

          SCIENCE Report      Lisa Wills
   Thermometer                Florencia medaano

MATERIALS:   SUN, Thermometer, window.

PROCEDURE:
1 WE Put the thermometer on the window.
2 Then we watched it go up.
3 After we moved it from the sun it went down.
4 but it did not go All the way down.
5 after it went back to 70 we Put it Back on the window.

RESULTs:
We found out the Thermometer goes up when it is By the sun and when it is Not By the sun it goes down.

reasoning. Scientific observations were made and appropriate conclusions drawn. A format for writing science reports was followed, including a list of necessary materials, a description of procedures, observations, and conclusions reached. Christina and Monica used a spring scale to weigh a variety of items (Figure 5–4c), a task which

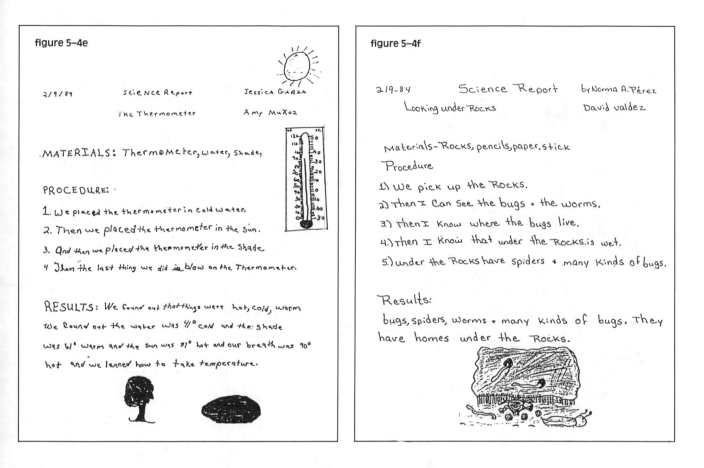

figure 5–4e

2/9/84        science Report          Jessica Garza

The Thermometer          Amy Muñoz

.MATERIALS: Thermometer, water, shade,

PROCEDURE: ·

1. We placed the thermometer in cold water.
2. Then we placed the thermometer in the sun.
3. And then we placed the thermometer in the shade.
4 Then the last thing we did is blow on the Thermometer.

RESULTS: We found out that things were hot, cold, warm
We found out the water was 41° cold and the shade
was 61° warm and the sun was 81° hot and our breath was 90°
hot and we learned how to take temperature.

figure 5–4f

2-19-84        Science Report        by Norma A. Pérez

Looking under Rocks        David Valdez

Materials - Rocks, pencils, paper, stick
Procedure
1.) We pick up the Rocks.
2.) Then I Can See the bugs + the worms.
3.) Then I Know where the bugs live.
4.) Then I Know that under the Rocks.is wet.
5.) under the Rocks have spiders + many Kinds of bugs.

Results:

bugs, spiders, worms + many Kinds of bugs, They
have homes under the Rocks.

also involved mathematical calculations. Lisa and Florencia examined
a thermometer (Figure 5–4d), as did Jessica and Amy (Figure 5–4e).
Norma and David went outside and looked under rocks (Figure 5–4f).

The science activities were so popular that the class asked to write
papers for a second volume. This time they used the projector

figure 5–5a

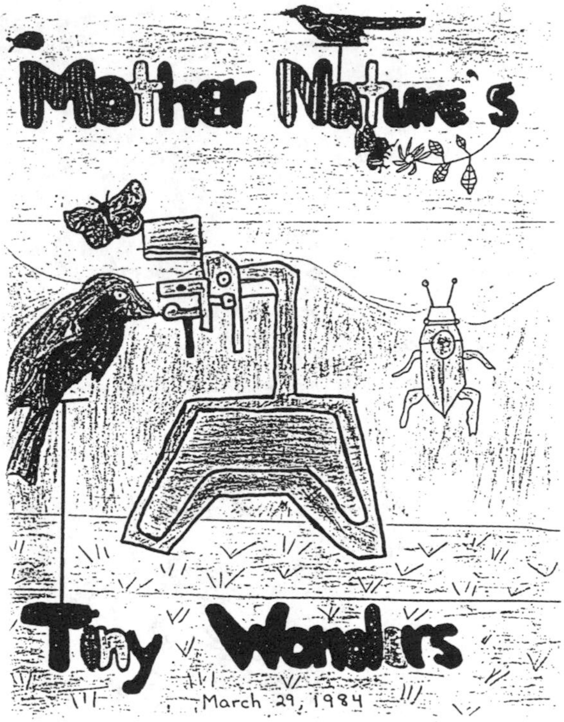

figure 5–5b

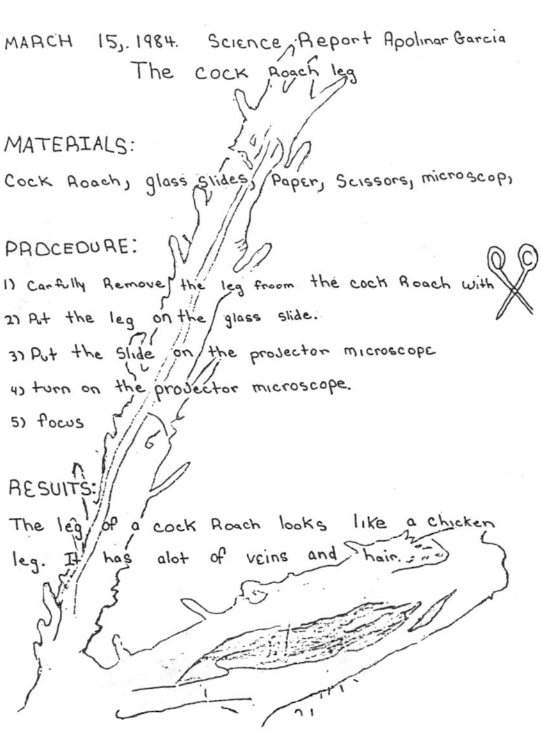

microscope and named their resulting book *Mother Nature's Tiny Wonders* (Figure 5–5a). Three reports from this book are reproduced in Figures 5–5b, 5–5c, and 5–5d.

Robert demonstrated that writing and reading were not isolated activities but activities integrated with the curriculum. Furthermore,

figure 5–5c

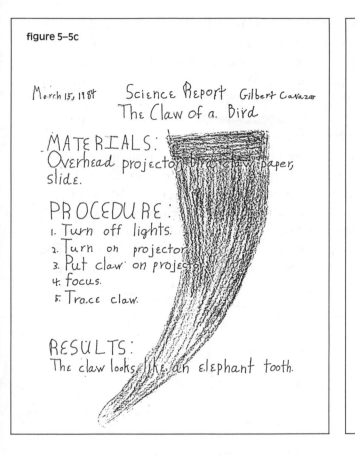

March 15, 1984   SCIENCE REPORT   Gilbert Cavazos
The Claw of a Bird

MATERIALS:
Overhead projector, bird claw, paper, slide.

PROCEDURE:
1. Turn off lights.
2. Turn on projector.
3. Put claw on projector.
4. Focus.
5. Trace claw.

RESULTS:
The claw looks like an elephant tooth.

figure 5–5d

March 15, 1984.   Science Report   Francisco Garza

A Sow Bug

MATERIALS:
paper, glass slide, over head projector microscope, sow bug.

PROCEDURE:
1) Put the sow bug on the glass slide.
2) Turn on the projector microscope.
3) Focus
4) Draw the picture.
5) Turn off the over head projector microscope.

RESULTS:
After a few minutes the sow bug die because it is hot to them and when they die they look like a circle. Putting the sow bug in the projector microscope and it is see big. They have hairs in the legs they look like tires in the back. The sow bug look like an armadillo.

writing and reading were not activities he required only of the children but activities he did along with them. He did not use writing to test factual knowledge; he elevated writing to the point where it taught. "In *making sense*," Moffett (1981) reminds us, "the writer is making knowledge" (148); and in a more recent publication, Moffett says,

"Though invented, we are told, about 3000 B.C., writing was discovered only about 1975—in American schools" (1989, 21). Writing to share knowledge, to make meaning, was what these students were about. We can learn from Donald Murray (1984), who says, "We do not write what we know so much as we write *to* know" (228).

For these children, writing about what they were learning led to learning. Learning comes from understanding, from a natural curiosity, from reading, from observing, from discussing, from questioning, from writing, from hands-on experiences with pieces of the world. While they were writing, reading, and increasing in confidence, the children were becoming better learners; their self-concepts were improving as they became literate. Their aspirations and projected futures evolved, changing with their experiences. Their IRI scores also improved. We will address and examine these aspirations in our last chapter.

# chapter

*Florencia dreams*
*new dreams*

*. . . transformation requires not only*
*a thorough analysis of the structure of schooling*
*and the ideology that informs it,*
*but it also necessitates a critical understanding*
*of the interdependence between schooling*
*and the sociocultural and political reality*
*of the society within which schools exist.*

Donaldo Macedo, *Literacies of Power*

As the date for the children's departure for the fields drew near, their abilities and confidence continued to increase. They enjoyed reading, being read to, and writing, putting their feelings, thoughts, aspirations, and knowledge onto paper. As we watched their engagement with learning, we gradually assumed—to employ Shirley Brice Heath's (1983) notion—the role of "doing" researchers (13). At the end of May, when we three sat down to discuss and assess the year, we concluded that granting sufficient time and extensive opportunities for reading and writing had enabled the class to progress and to acquire a positive academic self-concept and at the same time become a "literate community." The children also began to reflect metacognitive and metalinguistic awareness through literate discussions.

David Dillon (1987) says we often live in "an unjust, unfree, alienating, demeaning, and inhumane" world (135). Could writing and reading be the catalyst for changing a student's world of frustration to a world that is inviting, caring, and less threatening? Our intuition, reflection, observation, and assessment left us with the strong sense that the students were better and more contented learners. Because of our collaboration we believed Robert to be a better teacher in May than he was in August. The children taught us much about teaching and learning, even though it is difficult to point to any one catalytic variable. Each of us felt that a spirit, and an attitude, of "can do" began to permeate the students' sense of purpose, increasing their self-esteem, participation, and empowerment.

To us *empowerment* means choice, an affirmation of the home cultures and language of students—a self validation (see Freire 1970). Jim Cummins (1986, 1989, 1994, 1996) uses the verb empower to describe minority children who learn that they can learn. We believe children are born empowered, but school often strips empowerment from them. We also realize the danger of patriarchal notions of empowering others

# six

which can also be taken away. Students must empower themselves, but teachers are an important part of the process. Teachers must consciously and critically search out school mechanisms that disable students as they attempt to create a learning environment and relationship that allow students to achieve their innate potential with facility.

Empowerment will not result unless we address the mechanisms that withhold literacy and academic success from some learners. One mechanism is the perpetuation of literacy as the mere decoding of words, a mechanism which decontextualizes instruction and turns it into a skill-building sequence, from simple to complex. The employment in early reading instruction of word lists and texts that are often far removed from a child's contextual understanding of the world are instances of decontextualization. For these reasons, Freire (1983,1987) turns to a more inclusive concept of literacy and calls it "reading the word-world," a concept that correlates with Frank Smith's (*Understanding Reading,* 1994) cuing system of the word as including both *visual information* (information that is available on the page) and the cuing system of the world as *non-visual information,* information that is only available in the mind of the beginning reader as a result of his or her personal experiences. Ignoring the learner's non-visual knowledge while teaching the child to read creates a mechanism that will make it difficult (perhaps impossible) for her to learn to read. This instructional faux pas is convenient as we facilitate the reproduction of the status quo. According to Freire,

*One of the violences perpetrated by illiteracy is the suffocation of consciousness and the expressiveness of men and women who are forbidden the ability to read and write, thus limiting their capacity to write about their reading of the world*

*so that they can rethink their original reading of it. Even if illiteracy does not wipe out the socially created relationships between language, thought, and reality, illiteracy still remains a handicap and an obstacle to achieving full citizenship. (1998, 2)*

Once the child falls behind in reading the word, grade level bias becomes a second mechanism that ensures lower test scores for these learners and in turn provides educators with data to justify drawing racist conclusions about the intelligence of the child. Ironically, perhaps, learners from privileged classes remain relatively unharmed by these decontextualized approaches to literacy because they come to school at a level of emergent literacy which allows them to survive—despite the absence of context. The key difference between children from privileged class and those who are most harmed by this pedagogy is their relative exposure or lack of exposure to literate (written word) environments before the onset of schooling. Privileged children see their parents reading, are often read to by their parents, and grow up in print-rich environments. Children who "develop" reading problems in school often come from print-poor environments but not from environments where reading the world is also lacking. In fact, the opposite is more likely the case. Their environment is usually rich in opportunities to make good use of the context of the world around them. We would argue that the emergent literacy of these learners is rich in reading the world, and that reading instruction which ignores these strengths provides a mechanism for academic assassination.

These mechanisms, and others, coupled with transmission model instruction, ensure the success of some children and the failure of others—almost by zip code! Empowerment begins by providing pedagogical spaces where new skills emerge from developmentally appropriate experiences that use each learner's strengths as a foundation. When words used in instruction help to name the world in which the learner lives through learner-driven, generative reading and writing events in the classroom, the language of deficit is no longer a viable explanation as reading the word emerges organically from reading the world. Rather than buying into the language of deficit, we question the pedagogical validity—in other words, are we really teaching what we claim to be teaching? and if so, why aren't certain students learning?—of superimposed, reductionist approaches to reading the word.

Children can only empower themselves to the extent that teachers remove mechanisms that systematically produce failure. These theoretical and philosophical understandings lead to teachers empowering themselves, and, unfortunately, deskilled, technicist teachers cannot help students to participate in their own empowerment. In Farsi the saying goes, "A wolf does not give birth to a lamb."

Cummins's model of learning "emphasizes the development of higher-level cognitive skills and meaningful language use" rather than mere factual recall of discrete facts (1986, 28). He maintains that empowering children for school success is contingent on alterations in relationships among educators, communities, and minority children— the ways in which these groups see and perceive themselves. Specifically, Cummins examines three sets of interactions that can either lead to failure or promote success for minorities:

1. Intergroup power and status relations between dominated and dominating groups.
2. Relationships between the school and the minority community.
3. Classroom interactions between teachers and minority students.

Cummins believes that minority students, similar to our Mexican

American migrant children, in a society dominated by majority Anglo-American norms can either become empowered or disabled as a direct result of the interactions that occur at school. Cummins's thesis is much the same as Cazden's (1986), who identified barriers to excellence and equity for minority children, pointing to reductionist conceptions of language teaching, cultural differences between teacher expectations and child socialization, and inadequate communication between school and community and school and home.

As we have come to understand empowerment more clearly, the essence of what Robert accomplished came by providing opportunities for the children to take responsibility for their progress. An authentic oral and written conversation between the children and their teacher, who questioned, elaborated, prompted, guided, and facilitated instead of merely telling them what to do (Rogers 1971) set the stage for their self-empowerment. Robert taught and conducted the class in a collaborative learning context.

The students' problems began the first day they entered school, speaking a non-school language and bringing with them a culture so different from the one at school. Parents with little formal education who wanted their children to be educated but were intimidated by the school were not able to counter the effects of an alienating educational system. In tracing the children's steps from first to fifth grade, we found they were products of a *transmission model* of teaching, with the teacher at the center of instruction, initiating and controlling activities. Drills and exercises from workbooks had filled their days. Their teachers gave them information and then tested them on it. In effect, the metalanguage and discourse interactions necessary for reading, writing, and learning had been absent. Twenty-one of the students in this fifth-grade class read on the second-grade level, or lower, when the year began.

Robert challenged his students' overt attitudes toward school. He made it clear that he had a new set of expectations: The children could and would be active participants. Belief in success is at the heart of empowerment. A fluent Spanish speaker with a bicultural-bilingual family of his own, Robert employed both Spanish and English in the classroom. He introduced stories that represented folklore and oral traditions the children could relate to and identify with. His students, finding they were able to interact with him in Spanish and in English, gradually brought their home language and culture into the classroom. Robert changed his and their conceptions of school. Previous years' constant correction of errors had led to passivity, fear, and resistance. Their experiences had led them to believe that the teacher was the absolute authority and source for transmitting knowledge, which for them was unattainable. The disabling effect of this notion is apparent from Larry's response to Robert's query concerning writing: "I can't spell right. That's what bothers me about writing" (see Chapter 3).

Any change in Larry's and his classmates' attitudes could be brought about only by a radically different approach to teaching. Clearly, reteaching, remedial teaching, or grade retention were not answers. We have seen that many had already been retained, or remediated, and still had not learned. Clearly, they had to learn to read and write academically before any significant progress in school toward grade-level norms could occur.

## Creating, drafting, editing, and publishing

Improvement in writing does not occur just by commanding "Write!" A process and a structure for writing, as well as reasons to write, need to be provided. Before publishing, these students wrote a first draft. Robert joined with them in the process of writing, believing, along with

Graves (1981), that "the writing teacher, like the pottery teacher, must practice the craft alongside the students" (8). Robert and the children prepared drafts, which were then read aloud in small groups (the *helping circle*) of three to five classmates. Suggestions for revision made by the children were incorporated into subsequent drafts. Suggestions were positive and helpful, asking, for example, that the writer provide more detail or a specific reorganization of content. Robert read his own papers aloud to the entire class, asking for suggestions and comments; he then revised accordingly.

Quickly, these budding authors learned that all writers go through multiple drafts, and even the last draft may be subject to further revision, reorganization, or restatement as authors wrestle with getting it "just right" (Calkins 1986, 1994). As Hudleson (1986, 1989) and others have observed, second-language learners develop best as writers when they interact with readers of their writing. There is mounting evidence, furthermore, that peer readers exert stronger influence on each other's writing than teachers do. Most often, the third draft of these young authors went on to be edited for spelling and mechanics; the final version would then be illustrated and published.

For the editing process, an editing table (staffed by students) was set up, the mechanics of writing were reviewed, and the authors were given help with spelling, punctuation, and capitalization. Robert developed his students' sense of appropriate editing by showing how he edited his paper. Additional responsibilities of the editors included organizing the volume and providing a cover, table of contents, dedication and title page, and bibliography if needed. Publication of twenty-one volumes during the year gave all students extensive editing and publishing experience. Figure 6–1, taken from a book published in late spring, is a typical introductory page, citing previous class publications.

By May, the end of the school year, the set of twenty-one books

figure 6–1

Odds and Ends
   Mr. Bahruth's 5ᵗʰ Grade Class

Other books in print by the same authors:

Abecedario
Limited Edition
Love Letters
Autumn Leaves
The I Dare You Cookbook of Weird Recipes
Everything You Always Wanted to Know About Aliens...
      ...but were afraid to ask.
Our Favorites
International Alphabet Soup
Small Wonders and Magic Machines (Science Reports)
Uncle Sam's Biography
Great Expectations
Mother Nature's Tiny Wonders (Science Reports)
The New Improved I Dare You Cookbook of Weird Recipes
Conversation Pieces
The ABC Bestiary
Make-Believe Bestiary
The What Did U Say? Handbook of Idioms
Autobiographies of Not Yet Famous People
Our Outing
Dreamland


Copyright © May 24, 1984  The Farewell Edition
Printed in Texas "The Lone Star State" by:
López y Villarreal Publishers, Inc.
New York, London, Paris, Madrid, Pearsall.

Cover Layout and Design by Lisa Wills and Florencia Medrano

figure 6–2a

The Little Girl Who Loved Her Rabbit

Well My little sister is angry. Because she said not to touch her rabbit. And then when I came back she was crying. And then I said to My Mother and Father and my big sister that I was taking the rabbit to school. Tell My little sister. Because she was very in love with her rabbit.

by Irma pérez

figure 6–2b

THE DUCSH

By Irma "Hilda" Pérez

DUCISh are funny animals because. They have funny bodies the bodies is like ducks and the tail is like the fish. The ducsh eats insects, flower seeds and all kinds of food. The ducsh live in the water, in the forest, and the ducsh can be a pet too. THE color of the bodies is brown and the tail is red and some one has yellow bill and sometime has red and yellow. When the ducsh born. They not have the tail. When they has a week the tail has little and when they has 12 weeks they has big tail. .

reflected a broad range of writing categories: expressive, poetic or literary, and transactional or informational. The full set of publications provided a record of progress for the year, giving all the children a sense of achievement when they compared earlier volumes with those completed later. Figure 6–2a is a sample of Irma's writing early in the year. Her writing indicates minimal fluency and overuse of coordination (the *and . . . and . . . and* in her prose), a characteristic of early writing stages. Irma's writing at the end of the year (Figure 6–2b) shows significant progress. She clearly enjoys the topic of writing about make-believe animals for her contribution to *Make-Believe Bestiaries*. Irma, while still learning English, progressed significantly in fluency and in her ability to communicate to her audience ideas important to her. The progress from fall to spring also demonstrates considerable development in grammatical complexity and accuracy.

Clearly, Irma made substantial progress. She gained confidence in her ability to write—and she enjoyed the effects of writing. And she learned to read. She began the fifth grade at the primer (first-grade) level on the IRI; she ended the year at grade three-plus level, an indication of significant progress for one academic year. Even more remarkably, most of the class achieved the same increase in reading proficiency. More importantly, she and her classmates discovered the joy of being authors and the wonder and utility of reading and writing. In so doing, they took credit and responsibility for their success.

## The parents

We have seen that the students' previous academic failure appeared to be a result of complex interactions between home and school conditions. Poverty and limited formal education of parents had been employed as excuses that left the traditional pedagogy without meaning for the students, yet unquestioned. The children's teachers often did not respect the regional variety of Spanish spoken by the children. The parents were aware of the negative attitudes toward their Spanish dialect. Culturally, the parents accepted educators' conclusions out of deference. While they wanted and valued an education for their children, they knew of no way in which they could directly help. Nor did the teachers see the many ways parents could help were they to change their pedagogy (McCaleb 1994).

A turning point for the parents was the developing literacy of their children. Early in the year, the class became "hooked on books," looking forward to Fridays, the day when Robert introduced a number of new books by discussing title, author, dedication page, and then by reading a few pages from each aloud. At a point of high interest, he would close the book and ask whether anyone wanted to take it home for the weekend. Hands flew up. A book to take home over the weekend, or sometimes even to keep, was a reward for hard work during the week. Children prized these books. They also prized the books they had published and took them home on a rotating basis. The children shared this joy in writing, reading, and learning with their parents. As they read aloud to their parents, the parents increasingly noted the progress their children were making. One of Larry's later journal entries tells of his enthusiasm about taking books home and reading to his parents:

I'm Reading the new books
you brauf and I like
them and I'm going
to take one home so
I can Read on to my
Dad and mom.

*I'm reading the new books you brought. I like them, and I'm going to take one home so I can read it to my dad and mom.*

Parental encouragement bolstered the children's efforts to succeed. Quietly and unobtrusively, parents found a place in their children's education. Parents joined Robert as colleagues and aided their children, helping to foster reading, writing, and learning. Many parents commented on their children's eagerness to go to school in the morning, when previously it had been a battle of wills to get them going. The parents were not certain what Robert was doing, but they were pleased with the changes in attitude of their children.

## The tests

The state of Texas administers a battery of achievement tests yearly to all students in designated grades. Consistently low scores by migrant bilingual students have supported the position, held by many educators in the community, that these children have "learning disabilities" which prevent them from learning as quickly or expeditiously as monolingual English-proficient children. Classifying bilingual children from low socio-economic backgrounds as learning disabled is not uncommon in Texas. As Ortiz and Yates (1983) cite, Hispanic students in just Texas are overrepresented by a factor of 300 percent in the learning disabilities category. Learning disability is a widely used label confused with not knowing the English of the school well. A learning disability is one thing; a lack in the acquisition of English and English literacy is another. Failure to account for language and cultural variations in student populations continues to be a widespread problem in assessment. Low scores on previous achievement tests had resulted in extensive grade retention and remediation for the children in our class. Cummins (1986, 1989) maintains that faulty assessment instruments can legitimize the disabling of minority children. Elizabeth Schulz (1992) points to the disabling effects of testing and our obsession with standardized multiple-choice tests which impede educational innovation. She goes on to say they dominate the curriculum, shape classroom practice, sort students for tracking, and consume scarce time and money that could be much better spent (28).

We would argue that the real validity of these tests relates to their ability to measure privileged-class knowledge and ways of knowing. For this reason, they are biased and inappropriate for non-mainstreamed students. With Robert as their teacher, however, the children encountered a learning context that challenged the meaning and validity of low achievement scores. Robert saw a group of bright and potentially successful bilingual children who simply needed better conditions in school from the start. He used tests to measure their progress rather than their failure. He was aware of the grade-level bias, which ignored the reading levels of the students.

The students passed the required achievement tests. All were given the fifth-grade test, regardless. Reading was tested by the Informal Reading Inventory, which was routinely administered by the district. At the start of the year the class average equaled grade-level one; by the end of the year, the average had jumped to grade four (see Figure 6–3). Although most of the children were still below grade level, all had succeeded in improving their ability to read and write. Six of the twenty-two reached grade-level norms; one tested at grade-level seven. Even though the remainder scored below grade level, the average gain was substantial.

Such gains are gratifying: The children knew they had succeeded in

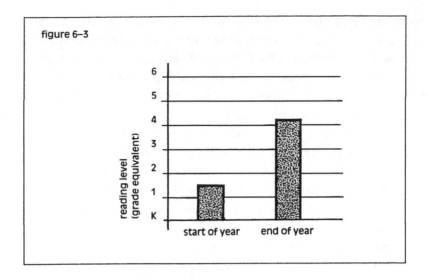

figure 6–3

learning, as did Robert and their parents. Gains of this magnitude demonstrate how students can turn around in achievement; they can indeed learn and succeed when the traditional mechanisms that cause failure are pedagogically neutralized.

## The children at work once again

Publishing continued as an integral part of classroom life. By spring, three books remained to be written and published: *Autobiographies of Not-Yet-Famous People*, a book that grew out of the children's reading of biographies of famous Americans; *Great Expectations*, a book generated by their desire to discuss and predict their futures; and *Odds and Ends*,

figure 6–4a

Table of Contents

figure 6–4a (continued)

Table of Contents

the last book, appropriately listed on the title page as the farewell edition.

*Odds and Ends* contained forty-six essays (see the table of contents reproduced in Figure 6–4a); some revisited themes from previous books while others were original. Many students included more than

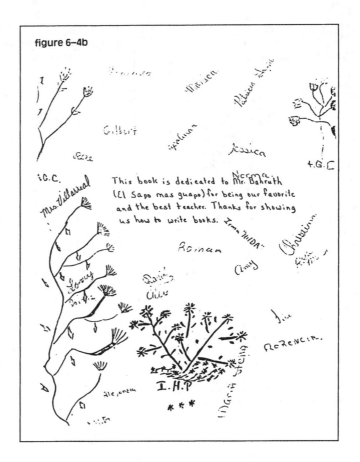

figure 6–4b

one paper; a few wrote as many as three. They secretly dedicated this final book to Robert (see Figure 6–4b).

*Odds and Ends* is not written around one theme—the students could include anything they wanted. Ten included papers about working. Irma writes of getting up in the morning and cleaning houses before going to

figure 6–4c

## THE WORK THAT I DO
### BY Irma "Hilda" Pérez

When I was lived in Nuevo, Laredo I worked in cleaning houses. I worked the seven days of the week but only two or three hours. But the first thing that I do is work on my house. Then I went to my work. Then at 1:00 O'clock I went to the school. Then I came from the school at 6:30 P.M. When I come I went to the another house at my work. When we came to Nuevo, Laredo, at Pearse-Texas. We worked on the field Peanut and first year, in this year I worked too. In this year I work cleaning houses, on the field Peanuts, baby sitter and Avon lady too. Sometimes I had all the work at the same time.

figure 6–4d

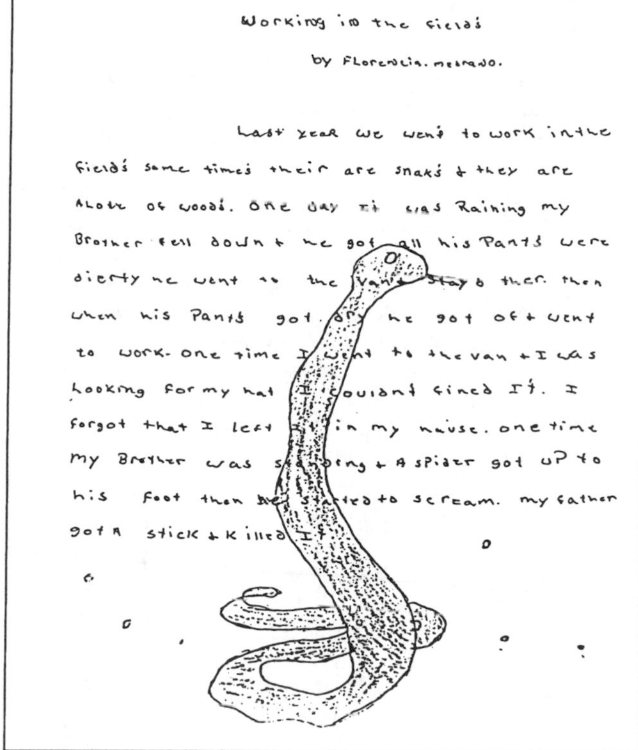

Working in the fields

by Florencia. medrano.

Last year we went to work in the fields some times their are snaks & they are alote of woods. One day it was Raining my Brother fell down & he got all his Pants were dierty he went to the Van. Stay's ther. then when his Pants got dry he got of & went to work. one time I went to the van & I was Looking for my hat I couldn't since it. I forgot that I left it in my house. one time my Brother was standing & A spider got up to his foot then he started to scream. my father got a stick & killed it.

school (Figure 6–4c). Others write of the work they did during vacations spent in the fields, the rodents and rattlesnakes they encountered, and their parents' difficulties in providing medical attention when needed. We have included three of these papers (Figures 6–4d, 6–4e, and 6–4f), which show how these children were performing the

figure 6–4e

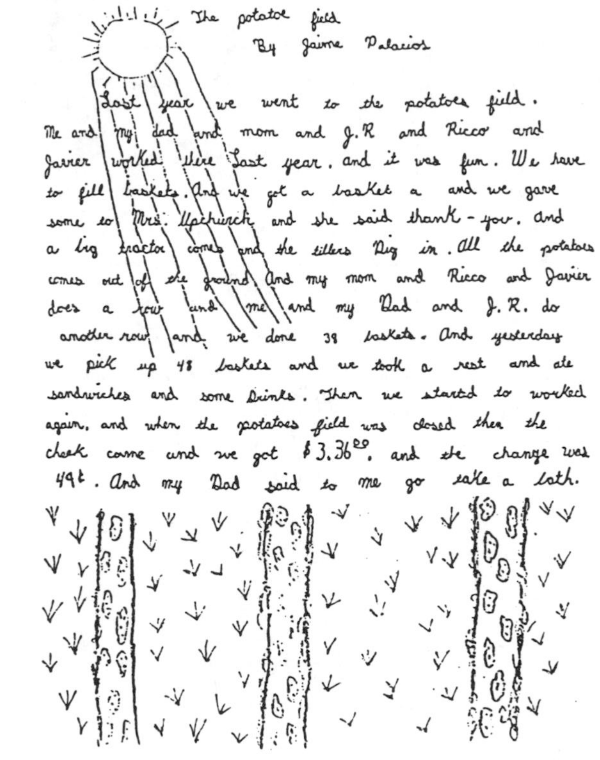

The potatoe field
By Jaime Palacios

Last year we went to the potatoes field. Me and my dad and mom and J.R and Ricco and Javier worked there last year. and it was fun. We have to fill baskets. And we got a basket a and we gave some to Mrs. Upchurch and she said thank-you. and a big tractor comes and the tillers Dig in. All the potatos comes out of the ground And my mom and Ricco and Javier does a row and me and my Dad and J.R. do another row and we done 39 baskets. And yesterday we pick up 48 baskets and we took a rest and ate sandwiches and some Drinks. Then we started to worked again. and when the potatos field was closed then the check came and we got $3.36⁰⁰. and the change was 49¢. And my Dad said to me go take a bath.

figure 6–4f

The Peanut Field
by: Jessica Garza

I started to work when I was in 3rd grade. I didn't know what to do. Then the first time I was real tired and we were singing. Once a snake bit my brother's shoe and he didn't move. His name is Joe. Then my grandma was taking care of my baby brother and we didn't like it because he always falls and my grandma has cement. And the I wanted to take care of him so I did and then my mom was not worried any more. I had to make the food and I stayed home with my two brothers and sister. And I gave my brother and sister sleep and they all slept. And last year we were working in Devine and the grass was long that was harder and we once went to eat at the Dairy Queen and it wasn't so big but it was pretty. And there was a rat that went in and out of the hole it was cute. We were real tired and we always went at 6.00am and went home at 4.00pm and my brothers played baseball

work of adults in the fields during the summer months as they harvested peanuts, cucumbers, pecans, onions, and potatoes. It is far from an easy life. Yet their essays also reflect the strong family values that helped them to face these challenges.

Many also wrote of their year in Robert's class. Irma reviews the books

figure 6–4g

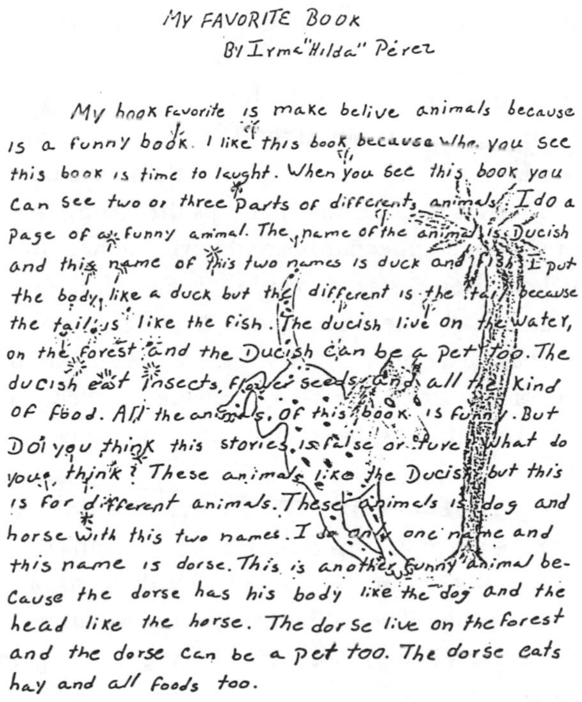
MY FAVORITE BOOK
By Irma "Hilda" Pérez
My book favorite is make belive animals because is a funny book. I like this book because whe you see this book is time to laught. When you see this book you can see two or three parts of differents animals. I do a page of a funny animal. The name of the animal is Ducish and this name of this two names is duck and fish. I put the body like a duck but the different is the tail because the tail is like the fish. The ducish live on the water, on the forest and the Ducish can be a pet too. The ducish eat insects, flower seeds and all the kind of food. All the animals of this book is funny. But Do you think this stories is false or ture? What do you think? These animals like the Ducish but this is for different animals. These animels is dog and horse with this two names. I se only one name and this name is dorse. This is another funny animal because the dorse has his body like the dog and the head like the horse. The dorse live on the forest and the dorse can be a pet too. The dorse eats hay and all foods too.

figure 6–4h

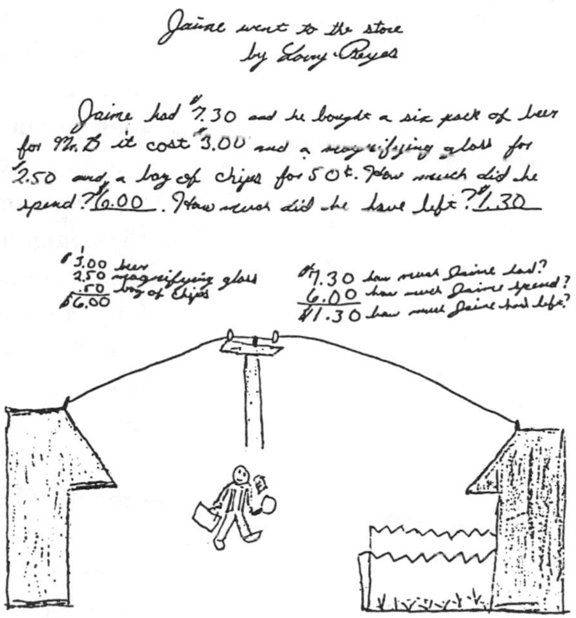
Jaime went to the store
by Larry Reyes
Jaime had $7.30 and he bought a six pack of beer for Mr. B it cost $3.00 and a magnifying glass for $2.50 and a bag of chips for 50¢. How much did he spend? $6.00. How much did he have left? $1.30
$3.00 beer
2.50 magnifying glass
.50 bag of chips
$6.00
$7.30 how much Jaime had?
6.00 how much Jaime spend?
$1.30 how much Jaime had left?

that the class published and lists her favorite (see Figure 6–4g), while Larry chose to create a word problem in his contribution (Figure 6–4h).

In all of these papers the strong voices of the students are heard. As readers of these papers, we can see them in the fields and can somewhat appreciate their difficult work. We can agree or disagree with Irma about which book is truly the best, or representative of the best. We can match wits with Larry and solve his word problem.

We could end here, with the test scores, with the final papers in the final book but . . .

*Great Expectations* contains papers about the future: "What do you want to be?" If education is even partially about the exploration and seeking out of alternatives in life, then these fifth-graders were on their way. They now had alternatives to consider. Perhaps the strongest evidence of and hope for changed expectations and performance for these migrant bilingual children rests in *Great Expectations*. It documents the students' dramatically altered attitudes. In the pages of this book, they write, "I want to be a doctor," "a lawyer," "a nurse," "a librarian," "a scientist," "a news reporter," "an artist," "a ballet dancer," "a teacher," always with the recognition that college and additional schooling will be necessary.

In her paper (Figure 6–5a), Florencia writes about a future in the orange groves. Oranges are a major crop grown in what Texans call "the Valley," that agriculturally rich strip of land in South Texas on the American side of the Rio Grande River. When asked if she planned to work in the orange groves for a living, Florencia answered, "I'm going to own the orange groves."

Gilbert, who began the year as a nonreader and ended the year reading at the third-grade level, grasped what becoming literate could mean when he wrote about becoming a scientist:

*When I grow up I would want to be a scientist. I want to work with test tubes and mix things. . . . And maybe someday I will discover a fluid for a skate board and I will be famous.*

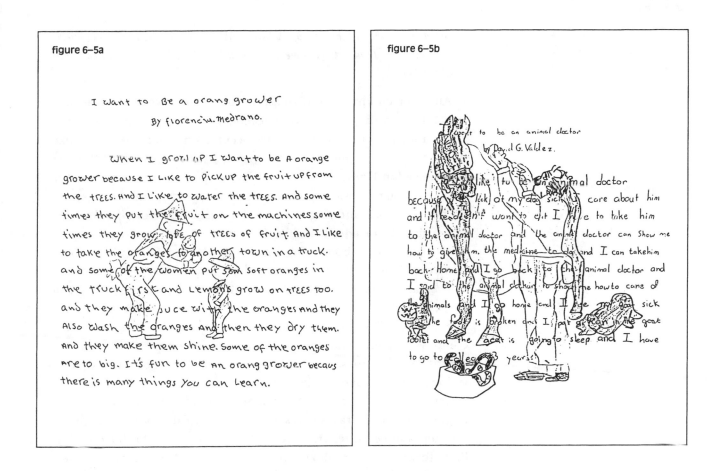

figure 6–5a

I want to Be a orang grower
By florencia. medrano.

When I grow up I want to be A orange grower because I Like to Pick up the fruit up from the trees. And I Like to water the trees. And some times they put the fruit on the machines some times they grow lofe of trees of fruit. And I Like to take the oranges to another town in a truck. and some of the women put som soft oranges in the truck first and Lemons grow on trees too. and they make juce with the oranges and they Also wash the oranges and then they dry them. And they make them shine. Some of the oranges are to big. It's fun to be An orang grower becaus there is many things you can Learn.

figure 6–5b

I went to be an animal doctor
by David G. Valdez.

I Like tu be an animal doctor because I lck at my dog sick I care about him and if he desn't wont to eat I lke to take him to the animal doctor and the animal doctor can Show me how to give him the medicine to do and I can takehim back home and I go back to the animal doctor and I said to the animal dcthar to show me howto care of the animals and I go home and I se my goat sick the food is broken and I pat green in the goat toolet and the goat is going to sleep and I have to go to college 3 years.

Norma's academic progress matched Gilbert's. Her success in fifth grade instilled in her the dream of becoming a teacher. In *Great Expectations,* she wrote:

*When I grow up I want to be a teacher because [it] is beautiful for me & I want to go to college. I like to take care of children. Al kind of children & I like math. I like to read. . . . I want to be someone special in the world. I want to be a bilingual teacher.*

All of the children had high aspirations: three (Norma, Patricia, and Rosa) decided they wanted to be teachers; two (Alejandra and Mónica) chose library science as their future occupation; others listed occupations as different from each other as animal doctor (see David's entry, reproduced in Figure 6–5b), nurse, lawyer, doctor, secretary, scientist, cowboy, airplane hostess, policeman, news reporter, ballet dancer, dairy farmer, musician, and singer. Some chose more than one profession: Florencia will consider teaching if she doesn't own orange groves; Norma also writes about being a nurse or a lawyer; Larry will choose between science and art.

Even as they considered and wrote about their futures in *Great Expectations*, the students looked at their pasts in *Autobiographies of Not-Yet-Famous People*. The children knew that they too had stories to tell and composed papers about their own lives. In these papers, we read of deaths, large families, broken families, hunger, alcoholism, and deprivations—but also about celebrations, sharing, and love. Florencia writes about the members of her family (Figure 6–6a). Francisco migrated from Piedras Niegras, Mexico, and writes about his eight brothers and two sisters (Figure 6–6b). Alex writes of his birth in Eagle Pass, Texas, across the Rio Grande from Piedras Niegras, and "in vacations" when his family travels to "Minisota" and "Wisconsen" (Figure 6–6c). Patricia continues the theme, common to most, of writing about her "big family" and her birth in Black Rocks (the translation of Piedras Niegras) (Figure 6–6d).

To know the children's past helps us to know them. All the students

figure 6–6a

ME And my family
by florencia. medRano.

I was born in Pearsall Texas in 1972 And my big brother is trying to be a dentist in chicago and my two brothers go to school and my other two brothers are working with my father. And my mother is showing me How to cook and wash the dishes and I have a sister in law she is 15 years old and she has a baby and her name is Beth and the baby's name is Patty and I writed her some letters and she writes me some letters too. And some time on the vacations we go to san antonio And one time we went to san antonio there was a carnival and we got on the spoky house and we gave Patty some Rides in the horses And one time we went to Cotulla and we went to my cousin's house their name's are Cindy, Elisa, adriana, And they have two twin brothers there names are Samuel + manuel and they are Big and we went bike Riding and my mother and father stayed with my Ants. And we went to the woods. And cindy is 11 years old and Elesa is 6 years old. And adrana is 4 years old + the two twin's are 1 years old And

figure 6–6a (continued)

ME And my family
by florencia. medrano.

My father's name is camilo And my mother's name is Felis.

had stories—histories—and their survival is chronicled in their words. Literacy became a tool for doing so (see Freire 1998). They wrote about their families and the close relationships they had with their siblings, and they also wrote about their "vacations" following the maturing of the crops from region to region. The autobiographies, the expecta-

figure 6–6b

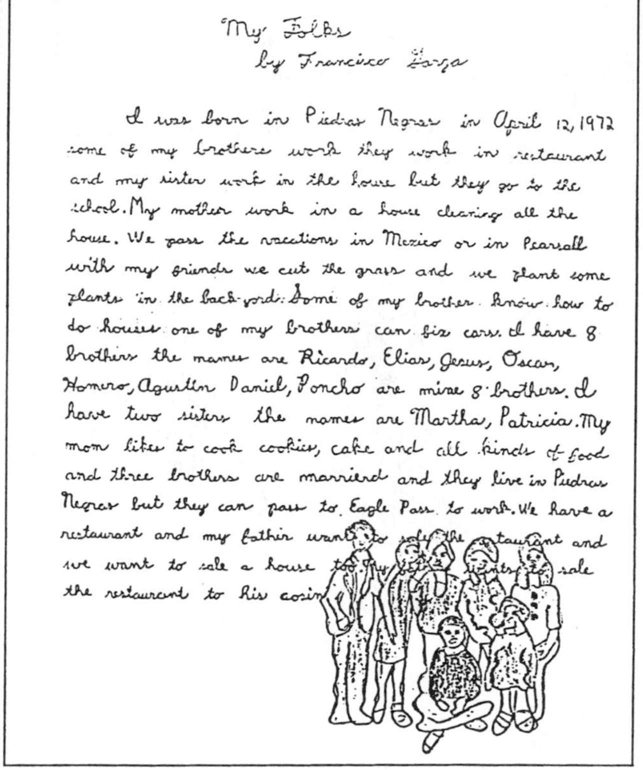

My Folks
by Francisco Zarza

I was born in Piedras Negras in April 12, 1972 some of my brothers work they work in restaurant and my sister work in the house but they go to the school. My mother work in a house cleaning all the house. We pass the vacations in Mexico or in Pearsall with my friends we cut the grass and we plant some plants in the back-yard. Some of my brother know how to do houses one of my brothers can fix cars. I have 8 brothers the names are Ricardo, Elias, Jesus, Oscar, Homero, Agustin Daniel, Poncho are mine 8 brothers. I have two sisters the names are Martha, Patricia. My mom likes to cook cookies, cake and all kinds of food and three brothers are married and they live in Piedras Negras but they can pass to Eagle Pass to work. We have a restaurant and my father want to sale the restaurant and we want to sale a house too my father sale the restaurant to his cousin

figure 6–6c

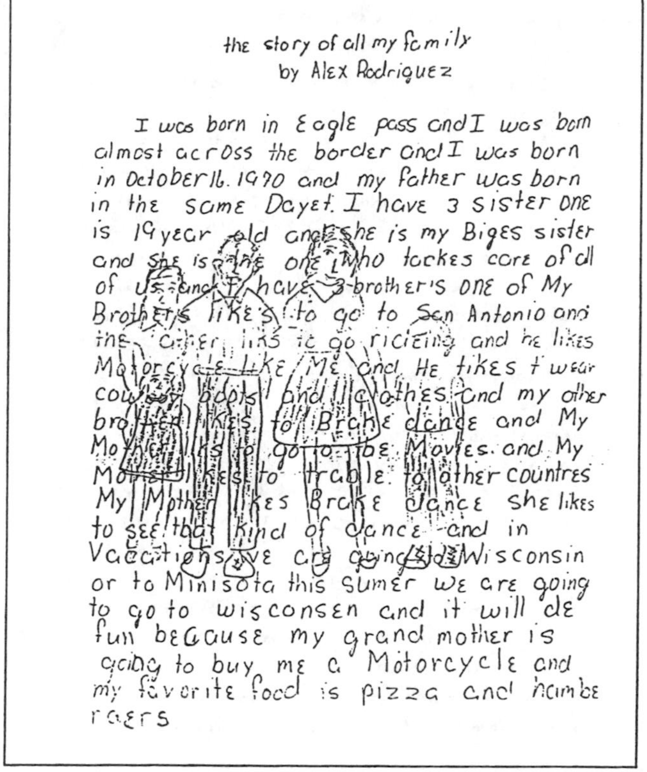

the story of all my family
by Alex Rodriguez

I was born in Eagle pass and I was born almost across the border and I was born in October 16. 1970 and my father was born in the same Dayet. I have 3 sister ONE is 19 year old and she is my Biges sister and she is the one who tackes care of all of us and I have 3 brother's ONE of My Brother's likes to go to San Antonio and the other liks te go ricieing and he likes Motorcyle like Me and He likes t wear cowboy boots and clothes and my other brother likes to Breke dance and My Mother likes to goto the Movies and My Mother likes to trable to other countres My Mother likes Breke dance she likes to see that kind of dance and in Vacations we are going to Wisconsin or to Minisota this sumer we are going to go to wisconsen and it will de fun becuase my grand mother is going to buy me a Motorcycle and my favorite food is pizza and hambe rgers

tions, all led us to share their lifeways, their rich but difficult experiences in merely surviving. Gilbert, Norma, Larry, and the others in their class still had a distance to travel to fully experience success in school. But one year had radically changed their perceptions of themselves. They could dream of continuing in school, of going on to colfigure 6–6d

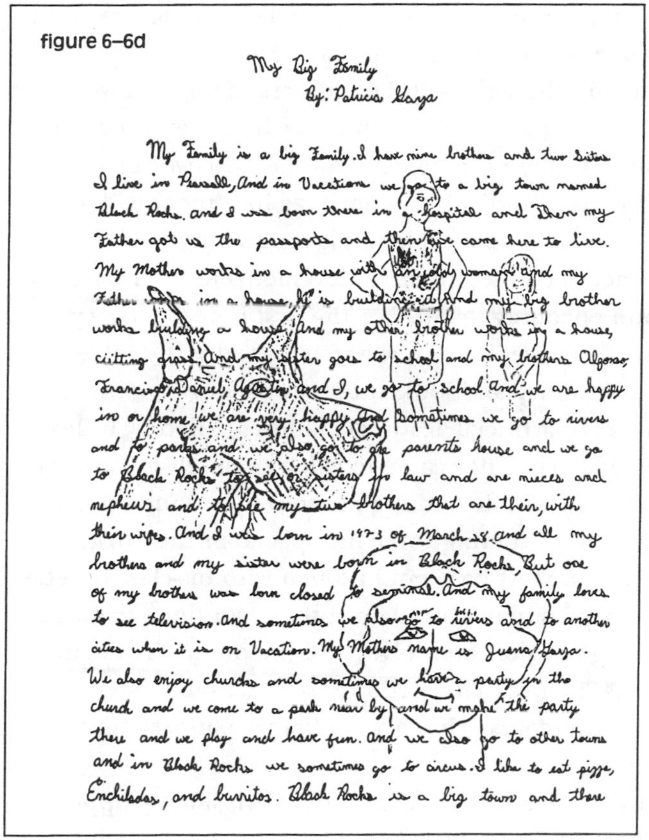

My Big Family
By: Patricia Garza

My Family is a big Family. I have nine brothers and two Sisters I live in Pearsall, And in Vacations we go to a big town named Black Rocks. and I was born there in a hospital and Then my Father got us the passports and then we came here to live. My Mother works in a house with an old woman and my Father works in a house, he is building it And my big brother works building a house And my other brother works in a house, cutting grass. And my sister goes to school and my brothers Alfonso, Francisco, Daniel, Agustin and I, we go to school. And we are happy in our home we are very happy And sometimes we go to rivers and to parks and we also go to are parents house and we go to Black Rocks to see or sisters in law and are nieces and nephews and to see my two brothers that are their, with their wifes. And I was born in 1973 of March 28 and all my brothers and my sister were born in Black Rocks, But one of my brothers was born closed to seminal. And my family loves to see television. And sometimes we also go to rivers and to another cities when it is on Vacation. My Mothers name is Juana Garza. We also enjoy churchs and sometimes we have a party in the church and we come to a park near by and we make the party there and we play and have fun. And we also go to other towns and in Black Rocks we sometimes go to circus. I like to eat pizza, Enchiladas, and burritos. Black Rocks is a big town and there

figure 6–6d (continued)

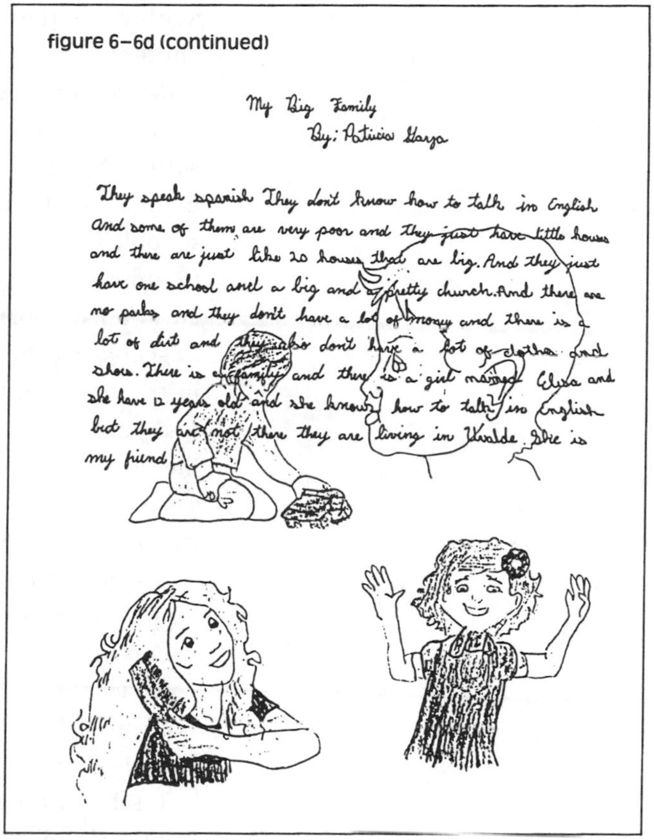

My Big Family
By: Patricia Garza

They speak spanish They don't know how to talk in English And some of them are very poor and they just have little houses and there are just like 20 houses that are big. And they just have one school and a big and a pretty church. And there are no parks and they don't have a lot of money and there is a lot of dirt and they also don't have a lot of clothes and shoes. There is a family and there is a girl named Elsa and she have 12 years old and she knows how to talk in English but they are not there they are living in Uvalde. She is my friend

lege, of becoming someone special. And they valued being bilingual and biliterate.

Their stories continue. Inability to function in English and their poverty and educational failures had been the expected facts of life by their teachers. As they discovered the value of talking, reading, and writing together in an atmosphere of support and encouragement, the children gained greater control over their learning. Their world widened and expanded. These sons and daughters of migrant workers, in this rural south Texas agricultural community, had been provided with pedagogical spaces where they were invited to discover how to incorporate their linguistic and cultural heritage into the world of school. They became excited about taking part in the interactions for learning. They had demonstrated their achievements to their parents and won support and encouragement. For the first time in many years of schooling they were succeeding. They had made educational leaders in the community take notice and look at them with new respect. They had jumped over years of artificial academic failure caused by inflexible, inappropriate pedagogy. They came to value themselves. And they were eager to move on to middle and high school. Continued schooling had a role to play in "becoming someone special in the world."

We do not end here. Robert has kept in touch with his class by letter and by visits whenever possible. A number of them continue to correspond with him, giving news of themselves and the others. They still consider their class as "family." They send report cards demonstrating successes; they share test scores. They are no longer children and have completed high school.

Of the original twenty-two fifth-graders, three girls later dropped out of school because of pregnancies. One boy, from a large family, dropped out for a year to help his dad start and continue a taco-stand business but returned to school, one year behind the others. Sadly, another, David, died in a car accident shortly after high school graduation. Those who left school continued working toward their GEDs. Some of them were in the gifted and talented classes in their high school. Most continue to live in the same South Texas area.

When they left that summer and piled into family cars headed toward the fields, they knew they could succeed. They knew they could learn. They knew how to take responsibility for their learning. They knew, as one of them summed up, "What it is about." And they still know—and we understand—*con cariño*!

# epilogue

*Literacy con Cariño* has been the story of a pedagogical shift that had significant impact on children, teachers, administrators, and parents. For us, the challenge continues, as we witness the success of our students—many of them first generation Americans. A number of the students knew some English, and all spoke Spanish at home. To be conversant in English and remain dominant in Spanish is not uncommon to the parents and their children in southwest Latino communities and particularly in a small isolated town sixty miles south of San Antonio. As Allen (1994) points out,

*many children in the United States whose home language is Spanish have lived in the country for some time, are surrounded by English, and have acquired aspects of English from television, in shops, and on playgrounds. (109)*

What they do not know is the language of survival in the school, academic competence in English.

In the first edition, we pointed to the failure and *drop-out* rate among these students as a result of their inability to use English for academic purposes. *Drop out* is the descriptor with which the educational community is most familiar; however, *drop out* semantically places the blame on the victims. The term has been challenged on exactly this point and the term *squeezed out* has been offered as more semantically appropriate, since it places the blame on systems that victimize, whether intentionally or not (Bahruth 1987).

There are many such scenarios where children are denied an education because they do not read and write English sufficiently well to pass into the next grade. For example, Rudolfo Anaya (1995), a victim of mainstream education, says:

*As a lifelong educator, I have argued for years that education must take into*

*account the culture of the individual child. No one can develop his full poten-*
*tial in an uncomfortable environment; one only learns to escape from an*
*uncomfortable environment as quickly as possible. (400)*

Many factors contributed to the success we experienced, but the following are key pedagogical adjustments that are essential:

1. For these children, learning means that books can be friends and learning can be enjoyable and invigorating. Only a few of these children have gone beyond high school, but a cycle of failure has been interrupted. Important for the success of children who live on the border of two languages are the following observations: These children did not understand (nor could they use) academic English that they would be expected to use in the middle school the following year; moreover, they did not write with facility. (Review Larry's initial attempts and David's undecipherable scrawl.) Therefore, we decided to have an interactive, occasionally noisy, classroom environment. A silent classroom is seldom a learning classroom. We encouraged noise (talking!), as long as the noise was about what they were learning. Our classroom was a beehive of productive, efficient activity.

2. Children use language as a tool for learning about their world. Kids ask questions; if they don't interact, the classroom may not offer much to them. We didn't teach language; we used language as a medium for other endeavors.

3. Language reveals social, economic, educational, ethnic, and regional identities. The children write about "The Work That I Do," by Irma, "Working in the Fields," by Florencia, "The Potato Fields," by Jaime, and "The Peanut Field," by Jessica. Teachers who wish to value students need to appreciate and build upon these experiences

and linguistic and cultural foundations. Freire (1998, 49) points out,

*When inexperienced middle-class teachers take teaching positions in periph-
eral areas of the city, class-specific tastes, values, language, discourse, syntax, semantics, everything about the students may seem contradictory to the
point of being shocking and frightening. It is necessary, however, that teachers understand that the students' syntax; their manners, tastes, and ways of
addressing teachers and colleagues; and the rules governing their fighting
and playing among themselves are all part of their **cultural identity**, which
never lacks an element of class. All that has to be accepted. Only as learners
recognize themselves democratically and see that their right to say 'I be' is
respected will they become able to learn the dominant grammatical reasons
why they should say 'I am.'*

Teachers, therefore, need to develop assignments that allow students opportunities to explore their worlds further. The acquisition
of academic competence is an active, structured, inductive process.
Therefore, focus should be more on learning than on teaching.
Emphasis should be on creating the pedagogical spaces that are conducive to fostering metalinguistic and metacognitive awareness.

4. What we learned is that by providing integrated and interesting
activities, children apprehend the utility of skills they are in the
process of mastering. Conversely, skill-driven, fragmented curricula,
complete with mastery tests, seem only to be measuring "temporary
custody" (Paley 1980) and ensure that the skills will be withheld.

There are no grades on our students' papers. Grades are just
inappropriate. They foster competition and reaffirm teacher author-
itarianism. We are interested in learning, and as soon as our students find they are not "at risk," they learn to write and read; they
listen to their classmates. Robert writes with them as a member of

the class; he directs the class and establishes goals, community structures, and routines.

Yet as teachers we are responsible for assessment. Marie Clay (1990, 295) asks:

*As a teacher, at what point are you interested in assessment? Probably it is pointless to try to measure this thing if the child has not yet started to learn it. Probably it is equally silly to take time out to assess it if the child can already complete the task perfectly. That leaves the period in between as a time that might be very interesting to the teacher. It could be the time when support or a hint about direction to move next might have the most effect. So, for the purposes of teaching, we might to be able to capture the half-right, half-wrong responding of our students and gain the maximum information on how to guide their next attempts or what opportunities we might provide to help them.*

Similarly, Dyson (1990) states:

*As professionals, as teachers, we listen to and read, not only the stories children write and tell, but the stories children are. We listen to how children talk to each other and to us; we observe them writing, responding, manipulating, contemplating. And, based on that listening and observing—that reading of each child-story, we make decisions about how Ruben, Sonia, or Jesse are progressing and how to best further each one's learning. Those decisions are influenced by our assumptions about the typical plot in the story of language development, about what should be expected. Over time, our perspectives may be enriched and made more complex by the many child-stories we read that shape our assumptions about what is "typical," "normal," or "natural." (194)*

5. Kids learn not from having their mistakes pointed out but through

timely nudges. Children make errors, many of which are developmental, that we would expect to appear; in fact, "Errors are the result of intelligence, not stupidity" (Scovel 1988). The "nudges" sometimes come from their peers (they read what others write and develop a taste for improved writing) and from Robert, who models his own writing, as well as talking about writing in writing workshops. For instance, in the science papers Gilbert is the first student who uses the imperative, often associated with scientific writing, and Robert holds Gilbert's work up as a model.

6. It is unrealistic to expect any group of learners to be on the same page at the same time. Developmental appropriateness is an individualized yardstick and the learner is often the best judge of what he or she is ready to take away from the discourse.

7. Teachers are not technicists. To put into practice the essentials above requires teachers to be intellectually engaged and reflective practitioners. Robert did not act in a vacuum. He was reading the research with a sense of obligation to improve pedagogy for students who he knew were bright and capable. He knew to question schooling rather than to accept the language of deficit to explain their previous failures.

These seven observations, or principles, led us to our activities and to our concern with bilingual children who do not do well in school, but who at the same time know their world. Journal writing is an important daily activity for rekindling literacy when too much "skill, drill, and kill" has extinguished the writing and reading flame. Skill building was a scaffold that came from reading and writing workshops where developmentally appropriate grammatical input, predicated on the teacher's attention to developmental characteristics of learner output, complements the free writing students practiced in their journals, where focus was on meaning rather than on form.

The improvement of writing skills revealed in the journals provided strong evidence that working on multiple drafts during writing workshop pays off. Robert de-emphasizes form, yet form consistently improves in journal writing. Conversely, contrived mastery level tests in a classroom that emphasized skill building seem to measure only that "temporary custody" (Paley 1980) of a skill which has been taught in decontextualized, unauthentic scope and sequence materials. Teachers need to learn how to read the interlanguage of their students and to use that information to provide developmentally appropriate instruction. Teachers know that skills taught and measured one day are often not employed the next. For example, words spelled correctly for spelling tests will not always be spelled correctly in subsequent writing activities.

Our book does not consist of a set of methods that teachers can follow like a lockstep but remains a text that portrays students learning in a literacy workshop milieu. We place reading and writing together, and the students are not aware of moving from reading to writing or from writing to reading.

We continue to read of research on bilingual children that says that these children may take five to seven years to complete the evolution of academic competence (Cummins 1994). We reply, unequivocally, that we don't have that much time. We face an urgency to teach successfully, in order to speed up and enhance the process of the acquisition of academic skills. Cummins's findings may be looking at the status quo of education, which is less than efficient in creating critical thinkers from any social, cultural or linguistic background, including privileged classes. A shift in paradigm makes for efficiency, which speeds up the acquisition by doing more in the classroom that is conducive to acquisition rather than conducive to withholding literacy and academic competence.

Finally, we need to address equal status issues in bilingual classrooms. The title of this book reiterates its significance. Spanish, English, and Tex-Mex are of equal status in the academic discourse of the classroom, even though most of the books we publish are in English. The code-switching dialect is valued as a natural expression of the two worlds these learners straddle. Stories are read and told in both Spanish and English throughout the year. As Lucy Calkins (1994) says,

*We cannot require our children to write beyond their capacity. We cannot assign them to be brilliant and original and deeply true. But we can create conditions in which this will happen. (251)*

And we have conditions where it will not happen: children in classrooms sitting in desks facing the front of the room, competing with their classmates for their place along the "normal curve"; teachers teaching in isolation, competing with colleagues for merit; principals competing with colleagues within their district; and superintendents, competing to avoid disgrace in the publication of statewide standardized test scores all represent prime examples of fragmentation, which cause distress in traditional schooling practices. Placing someone at the top requires someone to be at the bottom! Who is benefitting from this practice? Certainly not the children.

But change can occur when teacher-scholars come together as peers to examine the literature that is reshaping theory and philosophy, when together they design their classrooms and their pedagogy, when they produce significant improvements in the education of their students, and when teachers trust one another and their students. Too often the institutional response is to resort to fragmentation once more by breaking up the cadres of change—teachers like Robert—and assigning them, as though they were objects, to different schools throughout the district.

## Conclusion

The "Children of August," fifth-graders then, have graduated from high school and are pursuing life as adults. Several have gone to technical schools while a few have now entered community colleges and universities. Patricia, a member of that class, has completed four years of college at Boise State University and is seeking a degree in elementary bilingual education. The authors have made career changes. Robert graduated from The University of Texas with a Ph.D. in curriculum and instruction, with a bilingual and linguistics emphasis, and is a professor of education at Boise State University. Curt left The University of Texas at San Antonio and migrated to the northwest to join Robert at Boise State University, where he became chair of the Department of Elementary Education. Carolyn remains at The University of Texas at San Antonio. All authors still maintain an active agenda of research and interest in schools with language-minority needs.

The community where the children received their education has grown little. There is still one elementary, middle, and high school to accommodate the children of the community, whose members continue to migrate north to work in the fields. After the publication of *Literacy con Cariño*, the school board invited us to return to the community to participate in a symposium on bilingual education involving eight area school districts and to celebrate the success of Robert's fifth-grade class and *Literacy con Cariño*. We learned that Robert's colleagues were now focusing on reading and writing in a workshop approach modeled after the experiences in *Literacy con Cariño*. Some former migrant families are making the community their home year-round— Apolinar's family has opened a small restaurant.

We leave our readers with a "pedagogy of hope" (Freire 1997): that all kids, whatever their language background, previous school experiences, or station in life, can and deserve to learn. The conditions for learning are contained within *Literacy con Cariño*. Kids who at one time were being failed by the system are now active learners, because a teacher not only cared but presented in his classroom an opportunity for success. These students are learners, and they continued as learners in their school experiences. We understand that teachers must come to appreciate and incorporate what their students know into ways of educating them.

# references

Ada, Alma Flor. 1990. *A Magical Encounter.* Compton, CA: Santillana.

Allen, Virginia Garibaldi. 1994. "Selecting Materials for the Reading Instruction of ESL Children." In *Kids Come in All Languages,* 108–131. Newark, DE: International Reading Association.

Anaya, R. 1995. *The Anaya Reader.* New York: Warner Books.

Asher, James. 1985. "Motivating Children to Acquire Another Language." Oral presentation at the International Conference on Second/Foreign Language Acquisition by Children, Oklahoma City.

Atwell, Nancie. 1987. *In the Middle: Writing, Reading and Learning with Adolescents.* Portsmouth, NH: Boynton/Cook.

———. 1998. *In the Middle: New Understandings About Writing, Reading, and Learning, Second Edition.* Portsmouth, NH: Boynton/Cook.

Bahruth, Robert. 1987. "Dialogue Journals and the Acquisition of Spelling in a Bilingual Classroom," In *Dialogue,* ed. J. Peyton and J. Staton. Washington, D.C.: Center for Applied Linguistics. IV (1): 4.

Baugh, John. 1980. "A Reexamination of Black English Copula." In *Locating Language in Time and Space,* ed. William Labov. New York: Academic Press.

Beebe, Leslie M. 1988. *Issues in Second Language Acquisition.* New York: Newbury House.

Benitez, Diana. 1985. "A Bilingual Monoliterate? Implications for Reading Instruction." In *ERIC Clearinghouse on Languages and Linguistics* 8 (2): 1, 7.

Britton, James. 1970. *Language and Learning.* Baltimore: Penguin Books.

———. 1982. "Spectator Role and the Beginnings of Writing." In *What Writers Know,* ed. Martin Nystrand, 149–169. New York: Academic Press.

Byrd, Sam. 1996. Paper submitted for College of Education course in Bilingual Education, Boise State University.

Calkins, Lucy. 1986. *The Art of Teaching Writing.* Portsmouth, NH: Heinemann.

———. 1994. *The Art of Teaching Writing.* New ed. Portsmouth, NH: Heinemann.

Cazden, Courtney B. 1986. "ESL Teachers as Language Advocates for Children." In *Dialogue.* Washington, D.C.: Center for Applied Linguistics. 3 (2): 2–3.

Clay, Marie. 1990. "Research Currents: What is and What Might Be in Evaluation." *Language Arts* 67 (3): 288–298.

Cummins, Jim. 1986. "Empowering Minority Students: A Framework for Intervention." *Harvard Educational Review* 56 (1): 18–26.

———. 1989. *Empowering Minority Students*. Sacramento: California Association for Bilingual Education.

———. 1994. "The Acquisition of English as a Second Language." In *Kids Come in All Languages: Reading Instruction for ESL Students*, ed. Karen Spangenberg-Urbschat and Robert Pritchard, 36–62. Newark, DE: International Reading Association.

———. 1996. *Negotiating Identities: Education for Empowerment in a Diverse Society*. Ontario, CA: California Association for Bilingual Education.

Daiute, Colette. 1989. "Research Currents: Play and Learning to Write." *Language Arts* 66: 656–664.

Dillon, David. 1987. Dear Readers. *Language Arts* 64: 135.

Dyson, Anne Haas. 1990. "Research Currents: Diversity, Social Responsibility, and the Story of Literacy Development." *Language Arts* 67 (1): 192–205.

Edelsky, Carole. 1981. "From 'Jimosalsco' to '7 Naranjas se Calleron y el Arbol—EST—Triste en Lagrimas': Writing Development in a Bilingual Program." In *The Writing Needs of Linguistically Different Students*, ed. B. Cronnell. Los Alamitos, California: Southwest Research Laboratory.

Enright, D. Scott, and Mary Lou McCloskey. 1988. *Integrating English*. Reading, MA: Addison-Wesley.

Fox, Mem. 1987. "The Teacher Disguised as Writer, In Hot Pursuit of Literacy." *Language Arts* 64: 18–32.

Freire, P. 1970. *Pedagogy of the Oppressed*. New York: Continuum Press.

———. 1983. "The Importance of the Act of Reading." *The Journal of Education* 165: 5–11. Boston, MA: Boston University.

———. 1991. "Forward." In *An Unquiet Pedagogy: Transforming Practice in the English Classroom*, ed. Eleanor Kutz and Hephzibah Roskelly. Portsmouth, NH: Boynton/Cook.

————. 1997. *Pedagogy of the Heart*. New York: Continuum.

————. 1998. *Teachers as Cultural Workers: Letters to Those Who Dare Teach*. Boulder, CO: Westview Press.

Freire, P. and D. Macedo. 1987. *Literacy: Reading the Word and the World*. South Hedley, MA: Bergin and Garvey.

Fulwiler, Toby, ed. 1987. *The Journal Book*. Portsmouth, NH: Boynton/Cook.

Genishi, Celia. 1989. "Observing the Second Language Learner: An Example of Teachers' Learning." *Language Arts* 66: 509–515.

Gere, Anne R., ed. 1985. *Roots in Sawdust*. Urbana, IL: National Council of Teachers of English.

Graves, Donald H. 1981. Report. *Donald Graves in Australia*, ed. R. Walschc. Rosebery, Australia: Primary English Teaching Association.

————. 1983. *Writing: Teachers and children at work*. Portsmouth, NH: Heinemann.

Hansen, Jane. 1987. *When Writers Read*. Portsmouth, NH: Heinemann.

Heath, Shirley Brice. 1983. *Ways with Words*. New York: Cambridge University Press.

Hudelson, Sarah. 1986. "ESL Children's Writing: What We've Learned, What We're Learning." In *Children and ESL: Integrating Perspectives*, ed. Pat Rigg and D. Scott Enright, 25–53. Washington, D.C.: Teachers of English to Speakers of Other Languages.

————. 1989. *Write On: Children Writing in ESL*. Englewood Cliffs, NJ: Prentice Hall.

"Interactive Writing: Making Writing Meaningful for Language Minority Students." 1986. *National Association for Bilingual Education News* 10: 19, 21.

Jacobs, Suzanne E. 1984. "Investigative Writing: Practice and Principles." *Language Arts* 61: 356–363.

Kirby, Dan, and Tom Liner, with Ruth Vinz. 1988. *Inside Out*. 2d ed. Portsmouth, NH: Boynton/Cook.

Macedo, Donaldo. 1994. *Literacies of Power*. Boulder: Westview Press.

McCaleb, S.P. 1994. *Building Communities of Learners: A Collaboration Among Teachers, Students, Families and Community*. New York: St. Martin's Press.

Moffett, James. 1981. *Coming on Center: Essays in English Education*. Portsmouth, NH: Boynton/Cook.

———. 1989. "Introduction." In *Collaboration through Writing and Reading: Exploring Possibilities*, ed. Anne Haas Dyson. Urbana, IL: National Council of Teachers of English.

Murray, Donald M. 1984. *Write to Learn*. New York: Holt, Rinehart & Winston.

Nilsen, Don L. F., and Alleen P. Nilsen. 1978. *Language Play: An Introduction to Linguistics*. Rowley, MA: Newbury House.

Ortiz, Alma A., and J. R. Yates. 1983. "Incidence of Exceptionality Among Hispanics: Implications for Manpower Planning." *NABE Journal* 7: 41–54.

Payley. 1980. *Wally's Stories*. Cambridge, MA: Harvard University Press.

Rogers, Carl. 1971. "Forget You Are a Teacher." *The Education Digest* 37 (3): 17–19.

Schulz, Elizabeth. September 1992. "Enemy of Innovation." *Teacher Magazine* (4) 1: 28–31.

Scovel, Thomas. 1988. "Multiple Perspectives Make Singular Teaching." In *Issues in Second Language Acquisition*, ed. L. M. Beebe. New York: Newbury House.

Shuy, Roger. 1987a. "Dialogue as the Heart of Learning." *Language Arts* 64: 890–897.

Skutnabb-Kangas, T. and R. Phillipson, eds. 1994. *Linguistic Human Rights: Overcoming Linguistic Discrimination*. Berlin: Mouton de Gruyter.

Smith, Frank. 1983. *Essays into Literacy*. Portsmouth, NH: Heinemann.

———. 1988. *Joining the Literacy Club*. Portsmouth, NH: Heinemann.

———. 1994. *Writing and the Writer*. 2d ed. Hillsdale, NJ: Lawrence Erlbaum Associates.

———. 1994. *Understanding Reading*. 5th ed. Hillsdale, NJ: Lawrence Erlbaum Associates.

Stuckey, J. E. 1991. *The Violence of Literacy*. Portsmouth, NH: Heinemann.

Sucher, F., et al. [1978] 1982. *Informal Reading Inventory*. Oklahoma City: Economy Book Company.

Urzua, Carole. 1987. "'You Stopped Too Soon': Second Language Children Composing and Revising." *TESOL Quarterly* 21: 279–304.